# MALAGASY-ENGLISH
# ENGLISH-MALAGASY

## Dictionary and Phrasebook

# MALAGASY-ENGLISH
# ENGLISH-MALAGASY

## Dictionary and Phrasebook

**JANIE RASOLOSON**

**HIPPOCRENE BOOKS**
*New York*

For information, address:
HIPPOCRENE BOOKS, INC.
171 Madison Avenue
New York, NY 10016

www.hippocrenebooks.com

*Library of Congress Cataloging-In-Publication Data*

Rasoloson, Janie Noëlle, 1965-
    Malagasy-English, English-Malagasy : dictionary
and phrasebook / Janie Rasoloson.
        p.   cm.
ISBN-13: 978-0-7818-0843-X
ISBN-10: 0-7818-0843-X
    1. Malagasy language--Dictionaries--English.
2. English language--Dictionaries--Malagasy
3. Malagasy language--Conversation and phrase
books--English.

PL5376.R37   2001
499'.3321--dc21                          2001024279

THIS BOOK IS DEDICATED TO CHRISTIAN.

# CONTENTS

| | |
|---|---|
| PREFACE | IX |
| INTRODUCTION | 1 |
| ABBREVIATIONS | 3 |
| MALAGASY ALPHABET | 4 |
| PRONUNCIATION GUIDE | 5 |
| A BASIC GRAMMAR | 11 |
| MALAGASY-ENGLISH DICTIONARY | 25 |
| ENGLISH-MALAGASY DICTIONARY | 53 |
| MALAGASY PHRASEBOOK | 95 |
| FACTS ON MADAGASCAR | 169 |
| MAP OF MADAGASCAR AND MAYOTTE | 171 |

# PREFACE

$\mathcal{M}$alagasy is the language of Madagascar and the island of Mayotte (Comoro Islands), northwest of Madagascar across the Mozambique Channel. This dictionary and phrasebook contains an introduction to basic grammar, a two-way dictionary with over 2,000 entries, and a phrasebook, arranged in eighteen sections, presenting helpful simple phrases which deal with aspects of everyday life. The aim of this guide is to assist the traveler in his or her knowledge of the Malagasy language.

# INTRODUCTION

*M*alagasy refers not only to the approximately 14 million inhabitants of Madagascar but also to the language spoken throughout Madagascar and the island of Mayotte (Comoro Islands), northwest of Madagascar across the Mozambique Channel.

There are 21 Malagasy dialects. The Malagasy language which is described below is the so-called official Malagasy. Mainly spoken in the central highlands, this dialect is understood throughout Madagascar.

Malagasy is an Austronesian language with elements from Swahili, Bantu, Sanskrit, and Arabic. The Arabic influences on Malagasy are quite apparent: in the seventeenth century the Malagasy ethnic group *Antaimoro* (of the southeast coast) made use of the Arabic alphabet to write Malagasy. After 1820, the Malagasy king Radama I, who had learned to write Malagasy in Arabic characters, adopted the Roman script after British missionaries reproduced the Arabic writing in Roman.

Malagasy has numerous lexical borrowings from French and a few from English, a repercussion of sixty years of French occupancy and British influence.

French policy during the colonial period (1895–1960) was to assign the French language a privileged position over Malagasy (e.g. French in school, in newspapers and literature).

French was the official language in Madagascar, and this colonial blockade slowed down the development of a national language. Towards the end of the colonial occupation, even literate speakers regarded Malagasy as a foreign language.

After the independence in 1960 Malagasy acquired the status of an official language, besides French. School instruction switched into Malagasy, a process well-known as *malgachisation*. Its objective was to outline the national identity by promoting Malagasy language and culture. As Malagasy was gradually introduced into education, French lost its supremacy and instead became the first foreign language taught at school.

But in the early 1980s French was reinstated as the official school language, per the language policy of the minister of education at that time. So far *malgachisation* has been achieved at public primary school level only. The language of instruction after primary school switches to French. Private school education and university instruction remain essentially French. Despite this confusing language situation Malagasy has been the national language of Madagascar since a referendum passed in 1992.

# ABBREVIATIONS

| | |
|---|---|
| **ACC** | accusative |
| **adj.** | adjective |
| **adv.** | adverb |
| **art.** | article |
| **conj.** | conjunction |
| **dial.** | dialectal |
| **excl.** | exclusive |
| **GEN** | genitive |
| **incl.** | inclusive |
| **interj.** | interjection |
| **Lit.** | literal translation |
| **n.** | noun |
| **part.** | particle |
| **pl.** | plural |
| **POSS** | possessive |
| **prep.** | preposition |
| **pron.** | pronoun |
| **sing.** | singular |
| **subj.** | subject |
| **v.** | verb |
| *fr* | borrowings from French |
| *engl* | borrowings from English |

# MALAGASY ALPHABET

*T*he Malagasy alphabet contains 20 letters. The English consonants C, Q, W, and X as well as the vowel U do not exist in Malagasy.

A a
B bi
D dy
F èfo
G ge
H hàintso
I i
J ji
K ka
L èla
M èma
N èna
O o
P pe
R èra
S èso
T te
V ve
Y i grèka
Z zèdra

# PRONUNCIATION GUIDE

## ◆ Vowels

Malagasy words end in a vowel that is always very weakly pronounced, except for the final vowel "e" which is always stressed.

| Vowels | Approximate Pronunciation | Examples |
|--------|---------------------------|----------|
| o | "oo" in book | **mofo** bread |
| ô | "o" in more | **hôtely** hotel |
| e | "ea" in bread | **hena** meat |
| i/y | "ee" in three | **izy** she/he |
| a | "u" in custom | **masaka** ripe |

| Diphthongs | Approximate Pronunciation | Examples |
|---|---|---|
| ao | 1. "o" in more | **saosisy** sausage |
| | 2. final placing: "ow" in how | **manao** to do |
| ai, ay | "y" in my | **may** burnt |
| ei | "e" in elevation | **leitsy** form of address (between men only) |
| ia | 1. initial placing: "ya" in yard | **ianao** you |
| | 2. final placing: "i" in territorial | **lovia** plate |
| oa | 1. final placing: "oo" in look | **tokoa** really |
| | 2. otherwise: "o" in more | **foana** always, **fotoana** date |
| oy | "wi" in wizard | **Sotroy!** Drink! |

# ◆ Consonants

Malagasy has consonants and consonant clusters. The Malagasy consonants 'b', 'd', 'f', 'k', 'l', 'm', 'n', 'p', 't', and 'v' are pronounced like the English. The other consonants are spoken as follows:

| Consonants | Approximate Pronunciation | Examples |
|---|---|---|
| g | "g" in goose | **gaga** astonished |
| h | muted sound | **hena** [en] meat |
| j | "dz" in a**ds** | **jiro** light |
| r | "r" in rusk | **rano** water |
| s | "s" in salt | **sotro** spoon |

| Consonant Clusters | Approximate Pronunciation | Examples |
|---|---|---|
| dr | "dr" in **dr**agon | **gidr**o lemur |
| mb | "mb" in co**mb** | sa**mb**o ship |
| mp | 1. initial placing: like "p" in **p**age (m is silent) | **mp**ianatra pupil, student |
| | 2. in the middle of a word: "mp" in co**mp**ound | mana**mp**y to help |
| nd | "nd" in rou**nd** | ma**nd**o wet |
| ndr | "ndr" in lau**ndr**y | a**ndr**o day, weather |
| ng | "ng" in to**ng**ue | **ng**eza big |
| nj | "ndz" in ba**nds** | la**nj**a weight |
| nk | "nk" in dri**nk** | ma**nk**arary to make sick |
| nt | "nt" in au**nt** | A**nt**ananarivo (the capital of Madagascar) |
| ntr | "ntr" in cou**ntr**y | maha**ntr**a poor |
| nts | "n + ts" | a**nts**y knife |
| ts | "ts" in **ts**ar | **ts**ara good |
| tr | "tr" in **tr**uth | **tr**ano house |

# ◆ The Stress

The grave accent ` indicates the stressed syllable. It is not actually used in Malagasy orthography, with a few exceptions. Though an overview of the main stress usage is given, all stressed syllables will be marked with a grave accent ` for the reader's orientation.

◆ Most Malagasy words are stressed on the penultimate syllable: **hìta** to be seen, **mahìta** to see; **lomàno** swimming, **milomàno** to swim.

◆ The final vowels **a**, **o**, and **y** are uttered very weakly. The final "e" is always stressed: **mànana** to have, **misòtro** to drink, **màmy** sweet, **manomè** to give.

◆ Words ending in the weak final syllables **-ka**, **-tra**, or **-na** take stress on the antepenultimate syllable: **èfitra** room, **lòbaka** shirt, **làlana** street.

◆ In onomatopoetic words and in constructions based on them, the last syllable carries the stress: **vovò** wow wow, **mivovò** to bark.

◆ A stress shift one syllable to the right occurs in imperative constructions based on active verbs: **miàsa** to work, **Miasà!** Work!; **mitsàngana** to stand up, **Mitsangàna!** Stand up!

◆ In reduplication, the copied word in the second half carries the stress: **mòra** easy, cheap, **moramòra** somewhat easy, somewhat cheap.

◆ Demonstratives carry the stress on the last syllable: **ity** [itì] this; **iry** [irì] that.

There are numerous French words that are currently used in Malagasy. Either they do not have a Malagasy equivalent, or they are directly borrowed from French for everyday usage. These borrowings will be marked with *fr.* English borrowings are marked with *engl.*

# A BASIC GRAMMAR

*T*he author's aim is not to deal with aspects of Malagasy grammar in detail, but to provide the readers with elementary grammatical aspects of Malagasy, so as to help them understand and build simple sentences.

## ◆ Word Order

In a simple sentence, verbs are placed in the initial position: **verb + subject**.

**Manòratra àho.**
(write        I)
I write.

Malagasy is characterized by the basic word order V-O-S (verb-object-subject):

**Mamàky bòky àho.**
(read        book    I)
I read a book.

Adverbs of time such as 'today', 'tomorrow', 'yesterday', etc., occur in the final position: **verb + object + subject + adverb of time**.

**Nihàino radiò àho omàly.**
(listened  radio  I      yesterday)
I listened to the radio yesterday.

Local adverbs like 'here' and 'there' generally follow the verb if the sentence does not contain an object: **verb + local adverb + subject**. If the sentence contains an object, adverbs are placed either after the object or after the subject: **verb + object + local adverb + subject** *or* **verb + object + subject + local adverb**.

**Matòry àto ìzy.**
(sleep in here he/she/it)
He/she/it sleeps in here.

The meaning of the sentence does not change whether the subject occurs before or after the local adverb:

**Mànana tràno èto àho.**
(have house here I)
I have a house here.

**Mànana tràno àho èto.**
(have house I here)
I have a house here.

The verb "to be" does not exist in Malagasy: **adjective (v.) + person (subj.)** *or* **adjective (v.) + article + object (subj.).**

**Nòana àho.**
(hungry I)
I am hungry.

**Mànga ny lànitra.**
(blue the sky)
The sky is blue.

The adverb **tsy** put at the beginning of a sentence negates the sentence:

**Tsy** mànga ny lànitra.
The sky is **not** blue.

**Tsy** nòana àho.
I am **not** hungry.

## ◆ Personal Pronouns

Personal pronouns consist of full-form pronouns and clitic forms.

Malagasy has two forms of the first person singular pronoun, *àho* and *izàho*. Both can function as a nominative subject. The difference between *àho* and *izàho* is determined by word order. The former, *àho*, is used at the end of a sentence while the latter, *izàho*, is usually placed in initial position.

Malagasy differentiates between two forms of the first person plural: *isìka* 'we' includes the addressee while *izahày* 'we' excludes the addressee. The following table represents the personal pronouns:

| Pronouns | NOM | ACC | POSS/GEN (I) | (II) |
|---|---|---|---|---|
| 1st. sing. | izàho/àho | àhy | -ko | -o |
| 2nd. sing. | ianào | anào | -nào | -ào |
| 3rd. sing. | ìzy | àzy | -ny | -ny |
| 1st. pl. INCL. | isìka | antsìka | -ntsìka | -tsìka |
| 1st. pl. EXCL. | izahày | anày | -này | -ày |
| 2nd. pl. | ianarèo | anarèo | -narèo | -arèo |
| 3rd. pl. | ìzy irèo | àzy irèo | -n'izy irèo | -ny |

The indication of the possessive or the genitive relation in noun phrases is on the head noun:

tràno > trànonarèo
   (house_2nd. pl. GEN)
   your house

Hìtako ianào omàly.
(see_1st. sing. GEN you yesterday)
I saw you yesterday. (Lit.: You were seen by me yesterday.)

Malagasy has a genitive marker n' attached to the head noun. The enclitic pronouns are used to indicate possession of a nominal or to indicate the actor of a passive verb:

vòlan'    ny mpiàsa
(money_GEN  art. workers)
the workers' money

Vidìko    ny bòky.
(buy_1st sing. GEN art. book)
I buy the book. (Lit.: The book is bought by me.)

## ◆ Nouns

Malagasy nouns do not have a plural marker. Thus, a word like zanakarèo (from zanaka 'child(ren)' + -arèo 'your') may refer to the singular form 'your child' or to the plural form 'your children'.

Gender distinctions in Malagasy nouns are overtly marked with nominal modifiers. The gender markers are làhy and vàvy for 'male' and 'female', respectively. They follow the word they modify. Thus, from **ankìzy** 'child' is formed **ankìzilàhy** 'boy' (child male) and **ankìzivàvy** 'girl' (child female).

A common noun, such as *ankìzy* 'child(ren)', is usually preceded by the definite article *ny* 'the'.

Many proper nouns begin with the nominal prefixes **An-, Am-, Andria-, I-, Ra-, Ilai-** or **Ikàla-**. A proper noun that is the subject of a sentence and that does not begin with the nominal prefixes **I-, Ra-, Ilai-** or **Ikàla-**, is preceded by the nominal article *i*.

**Tsàra ny àndro.**
(nice *art.* weather)
The weather is nice.

**Miàsa i Nàivo.**
(work *art.* Nàivo)
Nàivo works/is working.

**Miàsa Ralày.**
(work Ralày)
Ralày works/is working.

The article *ilày* is used when the noun specified designates a referent already known by speaker and hearer:

**Ity    ilày bòky nomenào àhy.**
(this   that book  gave you me)
This is that book you gave me.

# ◆ Verbs

## Conjugation

Malagasy verbs are not conjugated:

**Miàsa àho.** I work.
**Miàsa ianào.** You work.
**Miàsa ìzy.** He/she/it works.
**Miàsa isìka.** We (incl.) work.
**Miàsa izahày.** We (excl.) work.
**Miàsa ianarèo.** You work.
**Miàsa izy irèo.** They work.

## Tenses

Malagasy verbs in the active voice generally begin with the prefix **m-**, which represents a present tense marker. In the past tense, **m-** is replaced by **n-** and in the future tense it is replaced by **h-**:

|           | Tense Marker | Examples            |
|-----------|--------------|---------------------|
| present   | m-           | <u>m</u>iàsa work   |
| past      | n-           | <u>n</u>iàsa worked |
| future    | h-           | <u>h</u>iàsa will work |

## The Imperative Mood

Imperatives are formed by the addition of the suffixes **-a, -o** or **-y** to the verb stem. Two imperative forms exist in Malagasy: the "active imperative" and "the passive imperative." Passive imperatives generally express more indirect requests, thus implying a higher degree of politeness, compared with active imperatives.

## *Active Imperative*

The active imperative is formed with the verb in the active form and the suffix **-a**. The active imperative generally follows the rules below. Notice the stress shift in the imperative verb.

1. If the verb does not end in the weak syllables **-ka, -tra** or **-na**, the suffix **-a** is added to the active form to build the active imperative:
mamàky to read, **Mamakìa!** Read!
manjòno to go fishing, **Manjonòa!** Go fishing!

2. If the verb ends in **-ka**, the consonant **-k-** of the last syllable **-ka** is replaced with **-h-**:
manòroka to kiss, **Manoròha!** Kiss!
manòmboka to begin, **Manombòha!** Begin!

3. In active verbs ending in **-tra, -tr-** of **-tra** is replaced by **-r-** or **-t-**:
manòratra to write, **Manoràta!** Write!
miànatra to learn, **Mianàra!** Learn!

4. When active verbs ending in **-na** are turned into the imperative form, the stress is shifted one syllable to the right:
mijànona to stop, **Mijanòna!** Stop!
manòmana to prepare, **Manomàna!** Prepare!

## Passive Imperative

1. The suffix **-o** or **-y** is added to the verb root to form the passive imperative. Generally, the suffix **-o** is used when the vowel "o" does not occur in the verb root:
   **manàsa** to wash, **sàsa** wash, **Sasào**! Wash!

2. The suffix **-y** is commonly used for the passive imperative when the verb root does not contain the vowel "i":
   **manòva** to change, **òva** change, **Ovày!** Change!

## Passive Voice

Passive verbs may be formed by the combination of a root with either the prefix **a-** or the suffixes **-ina** or **-ana**. Transitive verbs take a genitive marker followed by a genitive argument, which expresses the 'agent'. The nominative argument of passive verbs is non-agentive. For example, from the root **vàky** 'read' and the suffix **-ina** is formed the passive verb **vakìna** 'to be read'. In **Vakìn'i Rìna ny bòky**, the genitive marker is **n'**, the agent **i Rìna**, and the nominative argument is **ny bòky** 'the book'. Literally: the book is read by Rìna. The usual translation into English however is the active sentence: 'Rìna reads the book'.

# ◆ Adjectives

Adjectives have no gender distinction and no plural form. Like the active verbs, many adjectives beginning with **m-** may take the past tense marker **n-** and the future tense **h-**:

| | |
|---|---|
| present tense | **Maràry àho.**<br>(ill I)<br>I am ill. |
| past tense | **Naràry àho.**<br>(was ill I)<br>I was ill. |
| future tense | **Haràry àho.**<br>(will be ill I)<br>I will be ill. |

## Comparatives and Superlatives

For building equalities, five synonymous linkers may be used: **tahàka, òhatra, tòa, sahàla, mitòvy** 'as ... as'.

◆ same degree of comparison: **tahàka, òhatra, tòa, sahàla, mitòvy** as ... as

| **Kèly** | **sahàla** | **ny** | **nàmako** | **ìzy.** |
|---|---|---|---|---|
| (small | like | the | my friend | she) |

She is as small as my friend.

◆ comparative: **... noho** ...er than

◆ emphatic comparative: ... **kokòa noho** 'a little bit more ... than' *or* 'even ...er than...'.

Superlatives are built with the linker **... indrìndra** 'the most' or 'the ...est', and emphatic superlatives with the linker **tèna ... indrìndra** 'by far the ...est':

| **Ianào** | **no** | **làva** | **indrìndra.** |
|---|---|---|---|
| (you | *part.* | tall | the ...est) |

You are the tallest.

| **Ianào** | **no** | **tèna** | **làva** | **indrìndra.** |
|---|---|---|---|---|
| (you | *part.* | by far | tall | the ...est) |

You are by far the tallest.

All adjectives can be repeated in order to express intensification. The adjective forms remain unchanged and a linker (**dia**) is usually inserted in between the repeated forms:

**sàrotra dia sàrotra** very difficult indeed, **làva dia làva** very tall indeed.

## ◆ Adverbs

Adverbs are words that modify verbs, adjectives, other adverbs and sometimes sentences. They generally follow the element they modify, e.g. **Mitàfy <u>tsàra</u>** (dress well) 'to be well dressed' (postverbal), **vònona <u>vetivèty</u>** (ready a little while) 'ready in a little while' (postadjectival). A number of adverbs have the same forms as their adjectives, e.g. **fàtratra** 'amazing' vs. **fàtratra** 'amazingly'. But unlike adjectives, adverbs do not inflect.

Malagasy distinguishes the following main classes of adverbs:

*Manner adverbs*, to emphasize intensity or to express the absolute superlative: **tokòa, mihìtsy.**

*Comparing adverbs* (see above)

*Locative adverbs* are used to express place or the place where or wherein, for example **lavitra** 'far', **hatraiza hatraiza**, 'everywhere'.

Malagasy has also three locatives: proximal, medial and distal: **atsy, ato, aroa**, etc.

*Temporal adverbs* are used to express frequency, duration, time of occurance, e.g. **indraindrày** 'sometimes', **matètika** 'often', **èfa** 'already'.

A few temporal adverbs can be positioned freely within a sentence: after the verb, before the verb, between the verb and its complement, or it may occupy a final position: **Milomàno àho** (swim I). **Matètika milomàno àho./ Milomàno matètika àho./ Milomàno àho matètika.** All three sentences mean: 'I often swim'.

*Adverbial particles* are commonly used as answers: **eny** 'yes', **tsia** 'no'.

*Interrogative adverbs* are always used at the beginning of a sentence: **ovìana** 'when', **impìry** 'how often'.

# ◆ Questions

Interrogative sentences can be built by using interrogative pronouns:

◆ **Ìza** asks for a person.
  **Ìza   ianào?**
  (who  you)
  Who are you?

◆ **Ìnona** asks for a thing.
  **Ìnona ìo?**
  (what this)
  What is this?

◆ **Àiza** asks for a place.
  **Àiza   ìzy?**
  (where she/he)
  Where is she/he?

Interrogative sentences can also be formed by applying an interrogative intonation to an affirmative sentence, or by using the interrogative particle **ve** after the verb. The subject occurs at the end of the sentence:

**Miàsa   ianào?** *or* **Miàsa   ve   ianào?**
(work  you)          (work *part.* you)
Do you work?

**Miàsa   àiza   ianào?**
(work  where  you)
Where do you work?

**Manào   ìnona   ìzy irèo?**
(do      what    they)
What do they do?

If the interrogative pronoun *àiza* or *ìza* begins a sentence and is followed by the verb, the particle **no** is placed between the interrogative pronoun and the verb:

**Àiza    no    mipètraka ianào?**
(where *part.* live         you)
Where do you live?

## ◆ Reduplication

Only the elementary facts related to reduplication can be described here. Malagasy makes use of reduplication to encode semantic distinctions. Reduplication is based on copying the stem. Both adjectives and verbs may be reduplicated. The semantic effect of verbal reduplication is that of indicating manner (mainly iterativity or unmotivated/unsystematic event processing): **mihèrika** 'to look back' > **miherikèrika** 'to look behind one repeatedly', **mandròvitra** 'to tear' > **mandroviròvitra** 'to tear up into pieces'.

Adjectival reduplication is usually used for attenuation or for intensification of semantic effects. Disyllabic adjectives that do not end in **-ka, -tra,** or **-na** are copied in full form: **tèry** 'narrow' > **teritèry** 'somewhat narrow', **sìmba** 'broken' > **simbasìmba** 'somewhat broken', **mànta** 'unripe' > **mantamànta** 'somewhat unripe'. In some instances, adjectival reduplication may encode proximity to a final process: **vìta** ' finished' > **vitavìta** 'nearly finished', **fèno** 'full' > **fenofèno** 'nearly full'.

# MALAGASY-ENGLISH DICTIONARY

## A

**abidy** *n.* alphabet
**adàla** *adj.* crazy
**àdy** *n.* fighting; war
**àdy vàrotra** *n.* bargaining
**adìdy** *n.* responsibility
**àfaka** *adj.* free
**àfak'omàly** *n.* the day before yesterday
**àfo** *n.* fire
**afovòany** *adv.* in the middle
**àhitra** *n.* grass
**àho** *pron.* I
**àhy** *pron.* mine
**àina** *n.* life
**àiza** *adv.* where
**àizina** *n.* darkness
**akàiky** *prep.* near
**akànjo** *n.* clothing
**akòho** *n.* chicken
**akòndro** *n.* banana
**akòry?** How are you? (dial.)
**àla** *n.* forest
**alahàdy** *n.* Sunday
**alahèlo** *n.* sorrow
**alàina** *v.* to be fetched
**alakamìsy** *n.* Thursday
**alàmina** *v.* to be arranged
**alarobìa** *n.* Wednesday
**alèfa** *v.* to be sent
**Alemà** *n., adj.* German

**alèo** *v.* It is better
**àlina** *n.* night
**alòha** *prep.* before; *adj.* first
**ambanivòhitra** *n.* country
**ambàny** *prep.* under; down
**ambasadàoro** *n.* ambassador
**ambòa** *n.* dog
**ambòny** *prep.* above; up
**amìdy** *adj.* for sale
**àmin'** *prep.* with; at
**amòrona** *prep.* at the edge
**ampìtso** *adv.* tomorrow
**ampòndra** *n.* donkey
**àmpy** *adv.* enough
**anabàvy** *n.* the sister of a man
**anadàhy** *n.* the brother of a woman
**ànana** *n.* leafy vegetables
**anankirày** *adj.* one
**anào** *pron.* yours (sing.)
**anàrana** *n.* name
**anarèo** *pron.* yours
**anàty** *adv.* inside
**andavanàndro** *adv.* everyday
**andrahòina** *v.* to be cooked
**andrèfana** *n.* the west
**Andriamànitra** *n.* God
**Andriamatòa** *n.* mister
**àndro** *n.* day
**androàny** *adv.* today
**anèfa** *conj.* but
**angàha** *adv.* perhaps
**angatàhina** *v.* to be asked for
**anglìsy** *n., adj.* English
**aniè** *interj.* may it be so!
**anikehèo** *adv.* a short time ago
**anìo** *adv.* today

**ankapobèny** *adv.* generally

**ankehitrìny** *adv.* nowadays

**ankìzy** *n.* child (children)

**ànona** *n.* what-do-you-call-it

**àntitra** *adj.* aged; *n.* dark color

**antoàndro** *n.* daytime

**àntony** *n.* reason

**àntso** *n.* call

**àntsy** *n.* knife

**àny** *adv.* there (fairly far away, not visible)

**àoka** *adv.* enough!

**arabè** *n.* road

**arahàba** *n.* greeting

**àraka** *prep.* according to

**arètina** *n.* sickness

**arìvo** *n.* thousand

**àro** *n.* protection

**àry** *conj.* and

**àsa** *n.* work

**asabòtsy** *n.* Saturday

**atào** *v.* to be done

**àto** *adv.* here (close at hand)

**atòdy** *n.* egg

**atsìmo** *n.* the south

**atsinànana** *n.* the east

**àtsy** *adv.* there (not in sight)

**àty** *n.* liver

**aty** *adv.* here (not in sight)

**avàratra** *n.* the north

**avèla** *v.* to be left

**àvo** *adj.* high

**avokòa** *adv.* all

**àvy** *prep.* coming from; *n.* each one

**àza** *part.* don't

**àzo** *v.* got; allowed
**àzy** *prep.* his; her

# B

**bà** *n.* knitting; a kiss
**bà, bà kiràro** (optional) *n.* socks
**bàolina** *n.* ball
**baterìa** *n.* battery
**bètsaka** *adj., adv.* much
**bibikèly** *n.* an insect
**bìby** *n.* animal
**bisikilèty** *n.* bicycle
**boàty** *n.* a tin; a small carton
**bodofòtsy** *n.* blanket
**boribòry** *adj.* round
**bòzaka** *n.* grass

# D

**dahòlo** *adj.* altogether
**dìa** *adj.* wild; *n.* journey
**diavòlana** *n.* moonlight
**dìdy** *n.* order
**dìkany** *n.* translation, meaning
**dìmy** *adj.* five
**diòvina** *v.* to be cleaned
**dìso** *adj.* wrong
**ditè** *n.* tea
**divày** *n.* wine
**dòbo** *n.* pool
**dokotèra** *n.* doctor
**dòndrona** *adj.* clumsy
**dònina** *v.* to be knocked on

# E

**èfatra** *adj.* four
**èfitra** *n.* room
**eglìzy** *n.* church
**ekèna** *v.* to be agreed to; *interj.* okay!
**èla** *adj.* long (time)
**elanèlana** *n.* distance
**elektrisitè** *n.* electricity
**èlo** *n.* umbrella
**ènga** may ... !
**ènina** *adj.* six
**èntana** *n.* luggage
**èntina** *v.* to be carried
**èny** *adv.* yes
**èo** *adv.* there (near, in sight)
**èry** *adv.* there (quite far away, in sight)
**etsètra etsètra** *n.* and so forth
**èty** *adv.* here (fairly close)
**èzaka** *n.* effort

# F

**fa** *conj.* but; therefore
**fàdy** *n.* taboo
**fahadiòvana** *n.* cleanness
**fahagagàna** *n.* wonder
**fahamarìnana** *n.* truth
**faharòa** *adj.* second
**fahasalamàna** *n.* state of health
**fahasasàrana** *n.* tiredness
**fahatahòrana** *n.* fear
**fahatezèrana** *n.* anger
**fahatsiaròvana** *n.* the act of remembering;
    souvenirs

**fahavàratra** *n.* summer
**fahazotòana** *n.* zeal
**fahefàna** *n.* authority
**fahorìana** *n.* suffering
**fakan-tsàry** *n.* camera
**fàko** *n.* garbage
**faladìa** *n.* sole of the foot
**fàly** *adj.* happy
**famandrìhana** *n.* reservation
**famangìana** *n.* visit
**famantàrana** *n.* sign
**famantaranàndro** *n.* watch, clock
**famarànana** *n.* end
**fambolèna** *n.* agriculture
**famèrim-bòla** *n.* change
**famokàrana** *n.* agricultural production
**famonjèna** *n.* help
**fampandrenèsana** *n.* notice, announcement
**fampianàrana** *n.* teaching
**fampisehòana** *n.* exhibit
**fanadìnana** *n.* examination
**fanafàrana** *n.* ordering
**fanafòdy** *n.* medicine
**fanaintàinana** *n.* pain
**fànaka** *n.* furniture
**fanakalòzana** *n.* exchange
**fanalahìdy** *n.* key
**fanamarìnana** *n.* proof
**fanambadìana** *n.* marriage
**fanamboàrana** *n.* the act of arranging
**fanandràmana** *n.* tasting, testing
**fanantenàna** *n.* hope
**fanào** *n.* traditions, customs
**fanasàna** *n.* feast; invitation to a feast
**fandrìana** *n.* bed

**fanèfitra** *n.* vaccine
**fanekèna** *n.* agreement
**fangatàhana** *n.* request
**fànina** *adj.* dizzy
**fanirìana** *n.* wish
**fanjakàna** *n.* government
**fanomèzana** *n.* gift
**fanontanìana** *n.* question
**fàntatra** *v.* to be known
**fàsana** *n.* grave, tomb
**fàry** *n.* sugarcane
**fàsika** *n.* sand
**fatiàntoka** *n.* financial loss
**fe** *n.* thigh
**fehikìbo** *n.* belt
**fèo** *n.* sound
**fepètra** *n.* restriction
**fiàinana** *n.* life
**fiakàrana** *n.* climb
**fialàna** *n.* departure
**fiampangàna** *n.* accusation
**fianàrana** *n.* school
**fiangavìana** *n.* plea
**fiangònana** *n.* church
**fiarahabàna** *n.* greeting
**fiàra, fiàrakodìa** *n.* car
**fiàramanìdina** *n.* plane
**fiaròvana** *n.* protection
**fidìrana** *n.* entry
**fifalìana** *n.* happiness
**fifanaràhana** *n.* agreement
**fifidiànana** *n.* election
**fihàonana** *n.* meeting
**fihavànana** *n.* kinship, friendship
**fihavìana** *n.* origin

**fihògo** *n.* comb
**fikambànana** *n.* society
**filazàna** *n.* announcement
**filòha** *n.* head
**firàisana** *n.* union
**firavàna** *n.* the breaking up of a meeting
**firenèna** *n.* nation
**fisàorana** *n.* the act of thanking
**fitàovana** *n.* tools
**fitàratra** *n.* mirror
**fitatèrana** *n.* transport
**fitiàvana** *n.* love
**fitsabòana** *n.* medical care
**fitsaràna** *n.* court of law; judgement
**fitsìpika** *n.* rule
**fivalànana** *n.* excrement
**fivaròtana** *n.* shop
**fiverènana** *n.* return
**fizaràna** *n.* distribution
**fo** *n.* heart
**fòana** *adj., adv.* always; empty
**fòhy** *adj.* short
**fòlaka** *adj.* twisted
**fòlo** *adj.* ten
**fòmba** *n.* traditions

# G

**gàga** *adj.* astonished
**ganagàna** *n.* duck
**gàsy** *n., adj.* Malagasy
**gazèty** *n.* newspaper
**gìdro** *n.* lemur
**gìsa** *n.* goose
**governemànta** *n.* government

# H

**habè** *n.* size
**hàfa** *adj.* different
**hafanàna** *n.* heat
**hàfatra** *n.* message
**hafirìana?** *adv.* how long?
**hainàndro** *n.* sunshine
**hajàina** *v.* to be respected
**hànina** *n.* food
**hanoànana** *n.* hunger
**hàody!** *interj.* Hello! (asking for permission to come in)
**harìva** *n.* afternoon; evening
**hàrona** *n.* basket
**hasambàrana** *n.* happiness
**hasasàrana** *n.* fatigue
**hatrizày** *prep.* from the beginning
**hàvana** *n.* friend; relative
**havànana** *n.* the right side
**havìa** *n.* the left side
**hàzo** *n.* tree
**hèna** *n.* meat
**hènatra** *n.* shame
**hèndry** *adj.* wise
**herinàndro** *n.* week
**hèry** *n.* strength
**hetahèta** *n.* thirst
**hèty** *n.* scissors
**hèvitra** *n.* idea
**hìhy** *n.* gums
**hìra** *n.* song
**hìta** *v.* found; seen
**hòditra** *n.* skin
**hòfa** *n.* rent

**hòho** *n.* fingernail
**hòmana** *v.* to eat
**hòno** *v.* it is said
**hôpitàly** *n.* hospital

# I

**i** *art.* before proper names
**ianào** *pron.* you (sing.)
**ianarèo** *pron.* you (pl.)
**ihàny** *adv.* only
**ilàina** *v.* to be needed
**ilàozana** *v.* to be abandoned
**ilày** *art.* that
**indraindrày** *adv.* sometimes
**indrày** *adv.* again
**indrìndra** *adv.* especially
**ìnona?** *pron.* what?
**intsòny** *adv.* no more; no longer
**irày** *adj.* one
**irèny** *pron.* those (in sight)
**irèto** *pron.* these
**iry** *pron.* that (far away)
**ìsa** *n.* number; one
**isàorana** *v.* to be thanked
**isìka** *pron.* we (incl.)
**ìtsy** *pron.* that (not very close)
**ity** *pron.* this (close, in sight)
**ìva** *adv.* low
**ivèlany** *n.* outside
**ìza** *pron.* who
**izahày** *pron.* we (excl.)
**izàho** *pron.* I
**izào** *adv.* now
**ìzy** *pron.* he; she; it

# J

**jàmba** *adj.* blind
**jerèna** *v.* to be looked at
**jiolàhy** *n.* robber
**jìro** *n.* lamp; light
**jòno** *n.* fish bait
**joròfo** *n.* cloves

# K

**ka** *conj.* and so
**kabàry** *n.* ceremonial discourse
**kadòa** *n.* a tip for service rendered
**kafè** *n.* coffee
**kàikitra** *n.* bite; sting
**kàmo** *adj.* lazy
**kànkana** *n.* worm
**kàonty** *n.* bank account
**kàopy** *n.* cup
**karàma** *n.* wages
**karàoty** *n.* carrot
**kàratra** *n.* card
**karàzana** *n.* kind
**kàry** *n.* wild cat
**kasè** *n.* stamp
**kèly** *adj.* small
**kènda** *adj.* choked
**kèsika** *n.* box
**kiànja** *n.* public square
**kìbo** *n.* belly
**kidòro** *n.* mattress
**kìho** *n.* elbow
**kìla** *adj.* burnt up
**kilalào** *n.* toy

**kilàsy** *n.* classroom
**kilemàina** *adj.* handicapped
**kinìnina** *n.* quinine
**kìntana** *n.* star
**kiràro** *n.* shoes
**kisòa** *n.* pig
**kòa** *conj.* also
**kodiàrana** *n.* wheel
**kòhaka** *n.* cough
**komàndy** *n.* order
**komìty** *n.* committee
**kopìa** *n.* copy

# L

**lafarìnina** *n.* flour
**làfo** *adj.* sold; expensive
**lahàrana** *n.* line, row
**lahy** *adj.* male
**làkana** *n.* small boat
**lakilè** *n.* key
**lakozìa** *n.* kitchen
**làlam-by** *n.* railroad
**làlana** *n.* road
**lalandàva** *adv.* always
**làlan-drà** *n.* vein
**lalimoàra** *n.* cupboard
**làlina** *adj.* deep
**làmba** *n.* clothing
**làmbo** *n.* wild pig
**lànitra** *n.* sky
**lànja** *n.* weight
**lanònana** *n.* feast
**làny** *adj.* all gone; eaten up

**làoka** *n.* meat, fish, or vegetables eaten as rice
    garnish
**làsa** *adj.* gone
**lasàntsy** *n.* gasoline
**lasòpy** *n.* soup
**latàbatra** *n.* table
**làva** *adj.* long
**làvaka** *n.* hole
**làvina** *v.* to be denied
**làvitra** *adv.* far away
**lày** *n.* tent
**lehibè** *adj.* big; old
**lehilàhy** *n.* man
**lèla** *n.* tongue
**lèna** *adj.* wet
**lèsona** *n.* lesson
**lo** *adj.* spoiled
**lòaka** *n.* hole
**lòatra** *adv.* too much
**lòbaka** *n.* shirt
**lòha** *n.* head
**lohàlika** *n.* knee
**loharàno** *n.* spring (water)
**lohasàha** *n.* valley
**lòko** *n.* color
**lòlo** *n.* butterfly
**lomàno** *n.* swimming
**lovìa** *n.* plate
**lòza** *n.* danger

# M

**Madagasikàra** *n.* Madagascar
**madìo** *adj.* clean
**madìty** *adj.* sticky
**mafàna** *adj.* warm

**màfy** *adj.* hard, difficult
**mahafàly** *v.* to make happy
**mahafàntatra** *v.* to know
**mahafàty** *v.* to kill
**mahafinàritra** *v.* to please; *adj.* beautiful
**mahalàla** *v.* to know
**mahàndro** *v.* to cook
**mahàntra** *adj.* poor
**maharè** *v.* to hear
**mahàritra** *v.* to last
**mahasòa** *v.* to do good, to be good
**mahatsàpa** *v.* to feel
**mahatsiàro** *v.* to remember
**mahatsiràvina** *adj.* shocking
**mahàzo** *v.* to get
**mahèry** *adj.* strong
**mahìa** *adj.* thin
**mahìta** *v.* to see
**màina** *adj.* dry
**màinty** *adj.* black
**màitso** *adj.* green
**màivana** *adj.* light
**màizina** *adj.* dark
**màka** *v.* to take
**malagàsy** *n.*, *adj.* Malagasy
**malahèlo** *adj.* sad
**malàla** *adj.* dear, beloved
**malàlaka** *adj.* spacious
**malàza** *adj.* famous
**maloilòy** *adj.* nauseated
**màma** *n.* mum, mama, mother
**mamàfa** *v.* to sweep
**mamàha** *v.* to untie
**mamàky** *v.* to split; to read
**mamàly** *v.* to answer
**mamàna** *v.* to warm up

**mamàrana** *v.* to finish
**màmba** *n.* crocodile
**mambòatra** *v.* to repair
**mambòly** *v.* to plant
**mamèrina** *v.* to send back; to repeat
**mamètraka** *v.* to place, to set down
**mamìly** *v.* to drive
**mamìndra** *v.* to walk
**mamìta** *v.* to finish
**màmo** *adj.* drunk
**mamònjy** *v.* to save; to help
**mamòno** *v.* to kill
**mamòny** *v.* to blossom
**mampamàngy** *v.* to send greetings
**mampandrè** *v.* to announce
**mampiànatra** *v.* to teach
**mampiàsa** *v.* to use, to employ
**mampìditra** *v.* to bring in
**mampìndrana** *v.* to lend out
**mampisèho** *v.* to show
**màmy** *adj.* sweet
**manadìno** *v.* to forget
**manàfatra** *v.* to order (something)
**manàiky** *v.* to agree
**manaintàina** *adj.* sore
**manàja** *v.* to honor
**manakàiky** *v.* to approach
**manakàlo** *v.* to exchange
**manakàtona** *v.* to close
**manàla** *v.* to remove
**manamàrina** *v.* to prove
**manambàdy** *v.* to marry; *adj.* married
**manàmbatra** *v.* to add
**manàmpy** *v.* to help; to add to
**mànana** *v.* to have, to own

mananàsy *n.* pineapple
manàndrana *v.* to try; to taste
manantèna *v.* to hope
manào *v.* to do; to act
manàpaka *v.* to cut
manàraka *v.* to follow
manàry *v.* to lose
manàsa *v.* to wash; to invite; to sharpen (knife)
manatsàra *v.* to improve
manàvy *adj.* feverish
mandàinga *v.* to lie
mandàlo *v.* to pass by
mandàmina *v.* to arrange
mandànja *v.* to weigh
mandèfa *v.* to send
mandèha *v.* to go, to move
mandìmby *v.* to replace
mandìnika *v.* to examine
mandòsitra *v.* to run away
mandrakizày *adv.* forever
mandrày *v.* to receive
mandrè *v.* to hear
mandrèhitra *v.* to burn; to switch on
mandrìvotra *v.* to be windy
màndro *v.* to take a bath
mandròso *v.* to enter a house; to progress
Mandrosòa! Come in!
màndry *v.* to lie down
mangàlatra *v.* to steal, to rob
mangàtaka *v.* to beg; to ask for sth.
mangatsìaka *adj.* cold
mangetahèta *adj.* thirsty
mangìdy *adj.* bitter
mangìna *v.* to be silent
mangòtraka *v.* to boil; *adj.* boiled
mangòvitra *v.* to shiver

**manìdina** *v.* to fly; to pour out
**manìmba** *v.* to spoil
**Manìnona?** What's the matter?
**manìry** *v.* to wish; to grow
**manìsa** *v.* to count
**manjòno** *v.* to fish (with hook and line)
**mankaràry** *v.* to cause illness
**manòfa** *v.* to rent
**manòkatra** *v.* to open
**manòlo** *v.* to replace
**manomè** *v.* to give
**manòndro** *v.* to point at
**manontàny** *v.* to ask
**manòratra** *v.* to write
**manòro** *v.* to give advice
**manòroka** *v.* to kiss
**manòtra** *v.* to massage
**maràina** *n.* morning
**maràry** *adj.* ill
**maràtra** *adj.* injured
**marènina** *adj.* deaf
**màrina** *adj.* right; true
**màro** *adj.* many
**màsaka** *adj.* ripe; cooked
**màso** *n.* eye
**masoàndro** *n.* sun
**masoivòho** *n.* embassy; representative
**matàhotra** *v.* to be afraid of
**matètika** *adv.* often
**matòry** *v.* to sleep
**matsàtso** *adj.* tasteless
**màty** *adj.* dead
**mavèsatra** *adj.* heavy
**màvo** *adj.* yellow
**mày** *adj.* burnt; impatient
**mazàva** *adj.* light; clear

**mèna** *adj.* red
**mènaka** *n.* oil (any kind)
**mèty** *adj.* suitable; okay
**miàdy** *v.* to fight
**miàinga** *v.* to start off
**miàla** *v.* to leave
**mianadàhy** *v.* to be brother(s) and sister(s)
**miànaka** *v.* to be parent(s) and child(ren)
**miànatra** *v.* to learn; to study
**miandràikitra** *v.* to be responsible for
**miangàvy** *v.* to beg
**mianjèra** *v.* to fall down
**miàntso** *v.* to call
**miarahàba** *v.* to greet; to congratulate
**miàraka** *v.* to accompany
**miàsa** *v.* to work
**mibàta** *v.* to lift
**mìditra** *v.* to enter
**midòna** *v.* to bump
**mifankatìa** *v.* to love each/one another
**mifìdy** *v.* to choose
**mifòha** *v.* to wake up
**mihàino** *v.* to listen
**mihìra** *v.* to sing
**mihomèhy** *v.* to laugh
**mijànona** *v.* to stop
**mikàsa** *v.* to intend
**mikàtona** *v.* to be closed
**mikòhaka** *v.* to cough
**mìla** *v.* to need
**milalào** *v.* to play
**milàza** *v.* to say
**mìlina** *n.* engine; machine
**milomàno** *v.* to swim
**mìndrana** *v.* to borrow
**ministèra** *n.* ministry

**minìtra** *n.* minute (of time)
**mìno** *v.* to believe
**miòmana** *v.* to get ready
**miòva** *v.* to change
**mipètraka** *v.* to sit
**mirahalàhy** *v.* to be brothers
**mirahavàvy** *v.* to be sisters
**mirèsaka** *v.* to talk
**misakàfo** *v.* to eat a meal
**misàotra** *v.* to thank
**misàsa** *v.* to wash oneself
**misòkatra** *adj.* open
**misòratra** *v.* to register; *adj.* striped
**misòtro** *v.* to drink
**mìsy** *v.* there is, there are
**mitabatàba** *v.* to be noisy
**mitàdy** *v.* to look for
**mitèlina** *v.* to swallow
**mitèny** *v.* to speak
**mitòndra** *v.* to carry
**mitòvy** *adj.* equal
**mitsàbo** *v.* to give medical care
**mitsèna** *v.* to meet
**mitsìdika** *v.* to visit
**mitsìky** *v.* to smile
**mivàdy** *adj.* married
**mivèrina** *v.* to come back
**mivòaka** *v.* to go out
**mizàra** *v.* to share
**mòdy** *v.* to go home
**mòfo** *n.* bread
**mòka** *n.* mosquito
**mònina** *v.* to dwell
**mònja** *adv.* only
**mòra** *adj.* easy; cheap
**mpangàlatra** *n.* thief

**mpiànatra** *n.* student, pupil
**mpiàsa** *n.* employee
**mpitsàbo** *n.* doctor
**mpivàrotra** *n.* merchant

# N

**na** *conj.* or; either
**nahòana** *pron.* why?
**nàmana** *n.* friend
**ndào!** Let's go!
**nèny** *n.* mummy/mommy (address form)
**ngèza** *adj.* huge
**nìfy** *n.* tooth
**nòana** *v.* to be hungry
**Noèly** *n.* Christmas
**nòfy** *n.* dream
**nòho** *conj.* because of
**nòno** *n.* breasts
**nòsy** *n.* island
**ntàolo** *n.* ancestors
**ny** *art.* the

# O

**ô** *interj.* (exclamation used to address someone)
**òlana** *n.* problem
**òlombèlona** *n.* human being
**òlona** *n.* person
**omàly** *adv.* yesterday
**òmby** *n.* cow, ox
**òndana** *n.* pillow
**òndry** *n.* sheep
**òny** *n.* river

**òrana** *n.* rain
**òroka** *n.* kiss
**òrona** *n.* nose
**òsy** *n.* goat
**òtra** *n.* massage
**ovìana?** *pron.* when? (of past time)
**òvy** *n.* potatoes

# P

**pàiso** *n.* peach tree; peach
**palitào** *n.* jacket
**pàoma** *n.* apple
**pàositra** *n.* post office
**pàosy** *n.* pocket
**papàngo** *n.* hawk
**pasipàoro** *n.* passport
**patalòha** *n.* trousers
**pèjy** *n.* page (of a book)
**pènina** *n.* pen
**pensìly** *n.* pencil
**pèratra** *n.* ring (jewelry)
**pìso** *n.* cat
**pòizina** *n.* poison
**pôlìsy** *n.* policeman, police

# R

**Ra-** (prefix of personal names)
**ra** *n.* blood
**ràha** *conj.* when; if
**rahampìtso** *adv.* tomorrow
**raharàha** *n.* business; work
**ràhona** *n.* cloud
**rahovìana?** *adv.* when? (of future time)

**rajàko** *n.* monkey
**ràmbo** *n.* tail
**Ramosè** *n.* mister, Mr.
**ràno** *n.* water
**ranomàsina** *n.* sea
**ranomàso** *n.* tears
**ràozy** *n.* rose
**ràraka** *adj.* spilled, scattered
**raràna** *v.* to be prohibited
**ràtra** *n.* injury
**ràtsy** *adj.* bad; wicked
**ràva** *adj.* destroyed
**ràvina** *n.* leaf
**ravinàla** *n.* "the traveler's tree"
**rày** *n.* father
**ràzana** *n.* ancestor
**re** *v.* heard
**rèfy** *n.* measure
**rehèfa** *conj.* when
**rehètra** *adv.* all
**renivòhitra** *n.* capital (of a place)
**rèny** *n.* mother
**rèraka** *adj.* tired
**rèsaka** *n.* talk
**rìndrina** *n.* wall
**rirìnina** *n.* winter
**rìvotra** *n.* wind
**ròa** *adj.* two
**ronòno** *n.* milk
**ròvitra** *adj.* torn


# S


**sa** *conj.* or
**sàdy** *conj.* and also

**sàha** *n.* field; garden
**sahàdy** *adv.* already
**sahàla** *adv.* like (comparison)
**sahìrana** *adj.* busy
**sàingy** *conj.* however
**sàka** *n.* cat
**sakàfo** *n.* food; meal
**sakàiza** *n.* friend, companion
**salàdy** *n.* lettuce
**salàma** *adj.* healthy
**sàmbo** *n.* boat
**sàoka** *n.* chin
**saosìsy** *n.* sausage
**sàotra** *n.* gratitude
**sàrotra** *adj.* difficult
**sàry** *n.* picture
**sàsatra** *adj.* tired
**satrìa** *conj.* because
**sàtroka** *n.* hat
**sàzy** *n.* fine
**sekòly** *n.* school
**sèmpotra** out of breath
**serànana** *n.* harbor
**servièta** *n.* towel
**sèry** *n.* cold (sickness)
**sèza** *n.* chair
**sigàra** *n.* cigarette
**sìmba** *adj.* broken
**sìra** *n.* salt
**siramàmy** *n.* sugar
**sìsa** *n.* remnant
**sìvy** *adj.* nine
**sòa** *adj.* good; beautiful
**soavàly** *n.* horse
**sòkatra** *n.* turtle
**solomàso** *n.* glasses

**solontèna** *n.* representative
**sonìa** *n.* signature
**sòroka** *n.* shoulders
**sòtro** *n.* spoon
**sotrokèly** *n.* teaspoon
**sy** *conj.* and

# T

**ta-, te-** to want to (verb prefix)
**tàdy** *n.* rope
**tahàka** *adv.* like
**tàhotra** *n.* fear
**tàitra** *adj.* awake; startled
**tàiza?** *adv.* where? (of past time)
**takàlo** *n.* exchange
**talàta** *n.* Tuesday
**talè** *n.* director
**talòha** *adv.* before
**tamàna** *adj.* settled
**tàmpoka** *adv.* suddenly
**tàmy** *adj.* just arriving
**tànana** *n.* hand
**tanàna** *n.* town
**tandrèmana** *v.* to be cared for
**tànindràzana** *n.* native country
**tànjona** *n.* aim
**tantàra** *n.* story
**tantèly** *n.* honey; bee
**tantèraka** *adj.* completed; *adv.* totally
**tàny** *n.* soil; land
**tàolana** *n.* bone
**tàona** *n.* year
**taozàvatra** *n.* handicrafts
**tàpitra** *adj.* finished

taratàsy *n.* paper; letter
tarèhy *n.* face
tatavìa *n.* bladder
tàzo *n.* fever; malaria
telefàona *n.* telephone
telegràma *n.* telegram
tèlo *adj.* three
tèna *n.* body
tènda *n.* throat
tendrombòhitra *n.* mountain
tèraka *adj.* born
tèry *adj.* narrow
tèzitra *adj.* angry
tìa *v.* to love; to like
toèrana *n.* place
tòmpo *n.* owner; master
tònga *v.* to arrive
tòngotra *n.* foot; leg
totàly *n.* total
totòzy *n.* mouse
tovolàhy *n.* single young man
tovovàvy *n.* single young woman
tràno *n.* house
tràtra *n.* chest; *adj.* caught
tròndro *n.* fish
tsangambàto *n.* monument
tsàra *adj.* well, good
tsèlatra *n.* lightning
tsèna *n.* market
tsìa *adv.* no
tsìky *n.* smile
tsinày *n.* intestines
tsìndrona *n.* injection
tsìro *n.* taste
tsòtra *adj.* easy, simple; smooth
tsy *adv.* not

# V

**vàdy** *n.* spouse
**vahìny** *n.* stranger, foreigner
**vahòaka** *n.* people
**vàky** *adj.* broken
**valàhana** *n.* hip
**vàlo** *adj.* eight
**valòpy** *n.* envelope
**vaovào** *adj.* new; *n.* news
**vàratra** *n.* thunder
**varavàrana** *n.* door
**varìana** *adj.* distracted
**vàrotra** *n.* trade
**vàry** *n.* rice
**vàtana** *n.* body
**vàto** *n.* stone
**vatomàmy** *n.* sweets
**vàva** *n.* mouth
**vavènty** *adj.* large, big
**vàvy** *n.* female
**vazàha** *n.* (white-skinned) foreigner
**vehivàvy** *n.* woman
**vèlona** *adj.* alive, living
**vèra** *n.* glass
**vèry** *adj.* lost
**vy** *n.* iron
**vìdy** *n.* price
**vilàny** *n.* saucepan
**vilìa** *n.* plate
**vìta** *adj.* finished
**vìzana** *adj.* tired
**voalàvo** *n.* rat
**voalòboka** *n.* grapes
**voalòhany** *adj.* first
**voasàry** *n.* orange

**voatabìa** *n.* tomato
**voày** *n.* crocodile
**vòhitra** *n.* hill; village
**vòky** *adj.* filled
**vòla** *n.* money
**volafòtsy** *n., adj.* silver
**volamèna** *n., adj.* gold
**vòlana** *n.* moon; month
**vòlo** *n.* hair
**voninkàzo** *n.* flower
**vònona** *adj., adv.* ready
**vòrona** *n.* bird
**vorontsilòza** *n.* turkey
**vòzona** *n.* neck

# Z

**zàfy** *n.* grandchild
**zàitra** *n.* sewing
**zanabòla** *n.* interest (money)
**Zanahàry** *n.* God
**zànaka** *n.* child
**zàndry** *n.* younger brother or younger sister
**zaridàina** *n.* garden; park
**zàto** *adj.* hundred
**zatòvo** *n.* youth
**zàvatra** *n.* thing
**zàvona** *n.* fog
**zàza** *n.* child
**zìpo** *n.* skirt
**zòky** *n.* elder brother or elder sister
**zomà** *n.* Friday
**zòto** *n.* zeal

# ENGLISH-MALAGASY DICTIONARY

## A

**abandon** *v.* mandào
**ability** *n.* fahàizana
**able** *adj.* mahày; mahavìta
**about** *prep.* mòmba ny
**above** *prep.* ambòny
**abroad** *adj., adv.* àny ivèlany
**absent** *adj.* tsy tònga
**absorb** *v.* mitèlina
**absurd** *adj.* adàla
**accept** *v.* manàiky
**acceptable** *adj.* àzo ekèna
**accessible** *adj.* àzo alèha
**accident** *n.* lòza, aksidà *fr*
**accommodations** *n.* tràno ivantànana
**accompany** *v.* manàraka
**accomplish** *v.* mamìta
**ache** *n.* fanaintàinana
**acquaintance** *n.* olom-pàntatra
**across** *prep.* am-pìta
**add** *v.* manàmpy
**address** *n.* adirèsy
**adequate** *adj.* mifanàraka
**administration** *n.* fitondràn-draharàha
**adult** *n.* olon-dehibè
**advertisement** *n.* dòkam-bàrotra
**advice** *n.* tòrohèvitra
**advise** *v.* manòro hèvitra
**affair** *n.* raharàha
**afraid** *adj.* matàhotra

**after** *prep.* aorìana
**afternoon** *n.* tolakàndro
**afterward** *adv.* aorìan'izày
**again** *adv.* indrày
**against** *prep.* manòhitra
**age** *n.* tàona
**ago** *adv.* làsa
**agree** *v.* manàiky
**agreeable** *adj.* mahafinàritra
**agreement** *n.* fifanekèna, fifanaràhana
**agriculture** *n.* fambolèna
**ahead** *adj., adv.* alòha
**aid** *n.* fanampìana
**aim** *v.* mikèndry; *n.* tànjona
**air** *n.* rìvotra
**airplane** *n.* fiàramanìdina
**alcohol** *n.* alikàola
**alive** *adj.* vèlona
**all** *adj.* rehètra
**allow** *v.* mamèla
**allowance** *n.* anjàra vòla
**ally** *n.* hàvana (relatives); mpiàra-mitòlona
   (politics)
**almost** *adv.* sàika
**alone** *adj.* irèry
**aloud** *adj.* màfy
**alphabet** *n.* abidy
**already** *adv.* èfa
**also** *adv.* kòa
**although** *conj.* na dìa
**altitude** *n.* haavo ambònin'ny rànomàsina
**altogether** *adv.* avokòa
**always** *adv.* lalandàva
**amaze** *v.* mahagàga
**ambassador** *n.* ambasadàoro

**ambulance** *n.* fiàra mpitòndra maràry, ambulance *fr*
**among** *prep.* anìsany
**amount** *n.* habetsàhany
**amusement** *n.* fanalàna àndro
**ancestor** *n.* ràzana
**ancient** *adj.* àntitra
**and** *conj.* sy
**angry** *adj.* tèzitra
**animal** *n.* bìby
**ankle** *n.* kìtrokèly
**anniversary** *n.* aniversèra
**announce** *v.* manambàra
**announcement** *n.* fanambaràna
**another** *adj.* hàfa
**answer** *v.* mamàly; *n.* vàliny
**ant** *n.* vìtsika
**anybody** *pron.* na ìza na ìza
**anywhere** *pron.* na àiza na àiza
**apartment** *n.* appartement *fr*
**apologize** *v.* miàla tsìny
**appetite** *n.* fahazotòa-hòmana
**applause** *n.* fitehàfana
**apple** *n.* pàoma
**application** *n.* fangatàhana an-tsòratra
**appoint** *v.* manèndry
**appointment** *n.* fotòana
**appreciate** *v.* mankasìtraka
**approach** *v.* manakàiky
**appropriate** *adj.* mifanèntana
**approval** *n.* fanekèna
**approve** *v.* manàiky
**apricot** *n.* pàiso
**April** *n.* avrìly
**architect** *n.* architecte *fr*
**area** *n.* toèrana

**argue** *v.* miàdy hèvitra
**arm** *n.* sàndry
**armchair** *n.* sèza
**around** *adv.* manodìdina
**arrange** *v.* mandàmina
**arrest** *v.* misàmbotra
**arrival** *n.* fahatongàvana
**arrive** *v.* tònga
**art** *n.* zàva-kànto
**artist** *n.* artìsta
**as** *adv.* tahàka
**ash** *n.* lavènona
**ask** *v.* manontàny
**asleep** *adj.* matòry
**assembly** *n.* fivorìana
**assign** *v.* manèndry
**assist** *v.* manàmpy
**assistance** *n.* fanampìana
**assistant** *n.* mpanàmpy
**associate** *n.* mpiàra-miàsa
**association** *n.* fikambànana
**at** *prep.* ào (invisible); èo (visible); àny; èty
**attack** *v.* mamèly
**attempt** *v.* manàndrana
**attend** *v.* manàtrika
**attest** *v.* manamàrina
**auction** *n.* lavànty
**audience** *n.* mpijèry; mpihàino
**augment** *v.* mampitòmbo
**August** *n.* aogòsitra
**aunt** *n.* nenitòa
**author** *n.* mpanòratra
**authority** *n.* mànam-pahefàna
**authorization** *n.* fanomèzan-dàlana
**authorize** *v.* manomè alàlana
**autumn** *n.* fararàno

avenue *n.* arabè malàlaka
avoid *v.* misòroka
award *n.* valisòa
aware *adj.* mahatsàpa
away *adj.* tsy ào (not in)
awful *adj.* lòza
awkward *adj.* mikaviavìa

# B

baby *n.* zazakèly
back *n.* lamòsina
backbone *n.* hàzon-damòsina
bad *adj.* ràtsy
bag *n.* kitàpo
baggage *n.* èntana
bake *v.* mahàndro àmin'ny lafàoro
baker *n.* mpanào mòfo
balance *n.* mizàna
balcony *n.* lavaràngana
ball *n.* bàolina
bamboo *n.* bararàta
banana *n.* akòndro
bandit *n.* jiolàhy
bank *n.* bànky
bar *n.* bàra
barber *n.* mpanèty
barrier *n.* fèfy
basis *n.* fòtotra
basket *n.* hàrona
bathe *v.* màndro
bathing suit *n.* maillot de bain *fr*
bathroom *n.* tràno fandròna
battery *n.* baterìa
beach *n.* mòron-dranomàsina

bead *n.* vàkana
bean *n.* tsaramàso
beard *n.* volom-bàva
beast *n.* bìby
beautiful *adj.* tsàra tarèhy
because *conj.* satrìa
become *v.* manjàry
bed *n.* fandrìana
bedroom *n.* èfitra fandrìana
bedtime *n.* fotòana fatorìana
bee *n.* tantèly
beef *n.* henòmby
beer *n.* labièra
before *adv.* talòha; *prep.* alòa
beg *v.* miangàvy
begin *v.* manòmboka
beginning *n.* fiantombòhana
behind *prep.* aorìana
belief *n.* finòana
believe *v.* mìno
bell *n.* lakolòsy
belly *n.* kìbo
belong *v.* an'i
belt *n.* fehikìbo
bench *n.* dabilìo
beside *prep.* akàiky
better *adj., adv.* tsàra kokòa
between *prep.* anelanèlany
beyond *prep.* mihòatra
bicycle *n.* bisikilèta
big *adj.* lehibè
bill *n.* addition *fr*
bird *n.* vòrona
birthday *n.* aniversèra
birthplace *n.* toèrana nahateràhana
biscuit *n.* bisokì (cookie)

**bite** *v.* manàikitra; *n.* kàikitra
**black** *adj.* màinty
**blackberry** *n.* voaròihàzo
**blanket** *n.* bodofòtsy
**bleed** *v.* mandèha ra
**blind** *adj.* jàmba
**blood** *n.* ra
**blouse** *n.* blòzy
**blue** *adj.* mànga
**boat** *n.* làkana; sàmbo
**boil** *v.* mangòtraka
**bone** *n.* tàolana
**book** *n.* bòky
**border** *n.* sìsiny (edge); sìsin-tàny (between
    countries)
**boss** *n.* sèfo
**bottle** *n.* tavoahàngy
**bouquet** *n.* fehèzam-boninkàzo
**box** *n.* boàty
**boy** *n.* zazalàhy
**brain** *n.* ati-dòha
**branch** *n.* ràntsana (of finger); sàmpana (of a tree)
**break** *v.* manàpaka; *n.* fakàn-drìvotra (at school);
    *n.* fakàna àina (at work, at home)
**breakfast** *n.* sakàfo maràina, petit déjeuner *fr*
**breathe** *v.* miàina
**breathless** *adj.* sèmpotra
**bridge** *n.* tetèzana
**bring** *v.* mitòndra
**broadcast** *v.* mampièly vaovào
**broken** *adj.* tàpaka
**brother** *n.* rahalàhy (of a man); anadàhy (of a
    woman)
**brown** *adj.* vòlon-tàny
**bruise** *n.* màngana
**brush** *n.* miboròsy (hair, paint, wooden floor)

**buffet** n. buffet *fr*
**build** v. manambòatra
**bull** n. òmby
**bump** v. midòna; n. fifandònana
**bungalow** n. bungalow
**burglar** n. mpamàky tràno
**burn** v. mirèhatra (light, fire)
**bus** n. bus *fr*
**butterfly** n. lòlo
**button** n. bòkotra
**buy** v. mivìdy


# C

**cabbage** n. laisòa
**cake** n. mofomàmy
**call** v. miàntso; n. àntso
**camera** n. fàkan-tsàry
**canal** n. lakan-dràno
**candle** n. labozìa
**candy** n. vàtomàmy
**canoe** n. làkana
**cap** n. sàtroka làmba
**capital** n. renivòhitra
**car** n. fiàra, fiàrakodìa, tômôbìlina
**card** n. kàratra
**careful** *adj.* mitàndrina
**carrot** n. karàoty
**carry** v. mitòndra
**carving** n. sàry sòkitra
**cash** n. vòla tolo-bòsitra
**cat** n. sàka
**caterpillar** n. fandày
**cattle** n. bìby fiòmpy
**cause** n. àntony

**celebrate** *v.* mankalàza
**certificate** *n.* sertifikà
**chain** *n.* ròjo
**chair** *n.* sèza
**chairman** *n.* mpitàri-draharàha
**change** *v.* manòva; *v.* manakàlo vòla (money); *n.* vòla madìnika (coins)
**charcoal** *n.* àrina
**charge** *v.* mamèno (e.g. a lorry); *v.* mampandòa vòla (for a service); *v.* miampànga (accuse)
**charity** *n.* fiantràna
**chase** *v.* mihàza
**chat** *v.* miresadrèsaka; *n.* resadrèsaka
**chauffeur** *n.* saofèra
**cheap** *adj.* mòra
**check** *n.* sèky
**cheese** *n.* fromàzy
**chest** *n.* tràtra
**chew** *v.* mitsàko
**chick** *n.* akohokèly
**chicken** *n.* akòho
**chief** *n.* sèfo
**child** *n.* zàza, ankìzy
**chocolate** *n.* sokolà
**choice** *n.* safìdy
**choose** *v.* mifìdy
**church** *n.* fiangònana
**cider** *n.* rànom-pàoma
**cigarette** *n.* sigàra
**circulation** *n.* fifamoivoìzana
**circumstance** *n.* toe-jàvatra
**citizen** *n.* vahòakan'ny firenèna
**city** *n.* tanàn-dehibè
**civilian** *n.* òlon-tsòtra
**claim** *v.* mitàky
**class** *n.* kilàsy

**classify** *v.* mandàhatra
**clean** *v.* manadìo; *adj.* madìo
**clear** *adj.* mazàva
**clever** *adj.* kìnga sàina
**climate** *n.* toe-tàny
**climb** *v.* miànika
**clock** *n.* famataranàndro
**close** *v.* manìdy; *adj.* akàiky
**cloth** *n.* ravin-dàmba
**clothes** *n.* fitafiana
**cloud** *n.* ràhona
**club** *n.* fikambànana
**coast** *n.* mòron-dranomàsina
**cobbler** *n.* mpanào kiràro
**coconut** *n.* voanìo, coco *fr*
**coin** *n.* vòla madìnika
**cold** *adj.* mangatsìaka
**colleague** *n.* mpiara-miàsa
**collect** *v.* manàngona
**color** *n.* lòko
**comb** *n.* fihògo
**come** *v.* àvy, tònga
**comfortable** *adj.* mampiàdana
**command** *v.* mandìdy; *n.* dìdy
**commerce** *n.* vàrotra
**common** *adj.* fahìta
**communication** *n.* fifandràisana
**community** *n.* fokonòlona
**companion** *n.* nàmana
**company** *n.* fikambànam-bàrotra
**compare** *v.* mampitòvy
**complain** *v.* mitaràina
**complaint** *n.* fitaràinana
**complete** *v.* mamìta
**complicated** *adj.* sàrotra
**concept** *n.* hèvitra

**concert** *n.* fampisehòana
**conclude** *v.* mamàrana
**conference** *n.* konferànsa
**confidential** *adj.* tsiambàratèlo
**conflict** *n.* àdy
**congratulate** *v.* miarahàba
**connect** *v.* mampifandrày
**consul** *n.* màsoivòho
**contagious** *adj.* mifindra
**continue** *v.* mitòhy
**contract** *n.* fifanaràhana
**cook** *v.* mahàndro; *n.* mpahàndro
**cool** *adj.* mangatsiatsìaka
**cooperate** *v.* miàra-miàsa
**cooperation** *n.* fiaràha-miàsa
**copy** *n.* kopìa
**correct** *v.* manìtsy; *adj.* màrina
**cost** *n.* vìdiny
**costume** *n.* fitafìana
**couch** *n.* sèza làva
**cough** *v.* mikòhaka; *n.* kòhaka
**counselor** *n.* mpanòlo-tsàina
**country** *n.* firenèna
**courageous** *adj.* sàhy
**cousin** *n.* cousin(e) *fr.*
**cover** *v.* manàrona; *n.* sàrony
**crab** *n.* fòza
**crazy** *adj.* adàla
**creek** *n.* ràno mandèha
**criticize** *v.* manakìana
**crocodile** *n.* màmba, voày
**cry** *v.* mitomàny
**cup** *n.* kàopy
**cure** *v.* manasìtrana; *n.* fitsabòana
**currency** *n.* cours *fr*, vòla fampiàsa àmin'ny tàny
irày (Lit.: 'money used in a country')

**customer** *n.* mpivìdy
**cut** *v.* manàpaka; *adj.* tàpaka

# D

**dad** *n.* dàda
**daily** *adv.* isan'àndro
**damage** *v.* manìmba; *n.* sìmba
**dance** *v.* mandìhy; *n.* dìhy
**danger** *n.* lòza
**dangerous** *adj.* mampìdi-dòza
**dark** *adj.* màizina
**darling** *adj.* malàla
**date** *n.* fotòana (time)
**daughter** *n.* zànakavàvy
**day** *n.* àndro
**dead** *adj.* màty
**deaf** *adj.* marènina
**deal** *n.* vàrotra
**dear** *adj.* tìana
**debt** *n.* tròsa
**declare** *v.* milàza
**deep** *adj.* làlina
**defect** *n.* sìmba
**delay** *v.* manèmotra fotòana
**delicious** *adj.* matsìro
**dentist** *n.* mpanào nìfy
**deny** *v.* mandà
**departure** *n.* fiaingàna
**describe** *v.* manazàva
**description** *n.* fanazavàna
**desert** *n.* èfitra
**desire** *v.* manìry; *n.* fanirìana
**detail** *n.* antsipirìhiny
**develop** *v.* mampandròso

**development** *n.* fampandrosòana
**dictionary** *n.* diksionèra
**die** *v.* màty
**different** *adj.* sàmy hàfa
**difficult** *adj.* sàrotra
**dinner** *n.* sakàfo harìva
**director** *n.* talè
**disappear** *v.* manjàvona
**disaster** *n.* lòza
**discount** *n.* fihenàm-bìdy
**discuss** *v.* midìnika
**disease** *n.* arètina
**dish** *n.* lovìa
**dislike** *v.* tsy tìa
**distance** *n.* elanèlana
**distribute** *v.* mizàra
**divorce** *v.* misàraka; *n.* fisaràhana
**doctor** *n.* dokotèra
**document** *n.* antòntan-taratàsy
**door** *n.* varavàrana
**down** *prep.* ambàny
**dream** *v.* manonòfy; *n.* nòfy
**dress** *v.* miakànjo; *n.* akànjo
**drink** *v.* misòtro; *n.* fisòtro
**drive** *v.* mamìly
**driver** *n.* mpamìly, saofèra
**drunk** *adj.* màmo
**dry** *v.* manamàina; *adj.* màina
**duck** *n.* gàna
**dumb** *adj.* mòana
**duplicate** *n.* kopìa
**duration** *n.* faharètana
**during** *prep.* mandrìtra
**dusk** *n.* takarìva
**dust** *n.* vòvoka

# E

**each** *adv.* àvy
**ear** *n.* sòfina
**early** *adv.* alòha
**earth** *n.* tàny
**east** *adj.* atsinànana
**easy** *adj.* mòra
**eat** *v.* misakàfo (to have breakfast, lunch, or dinner); mihìnana (to eat sth)
**economy** *n.* toè-karèna
**educate** *v.* mampiànatra
**education** *n.* fampianàrana
**effort** *n.* èzaka
**egg** *n.* atòdy
**eight** *adj.* vàlo
**either** *conj.* na; na … na
**elbow** *n.* kìho
**election** *n.* fifidiànana
**else** *adv.* hàfa
**embassy** *n.* ambasàdy
**employ** *v.* mampiàsa
**employee** *n.* mpiàsa
**empty** *adj.* fòana
**end** *v.* mamàrana; *n.* fàrany
**engine** *n.* mìlina
**enjoy** *v.* mifàly
**enough** *adj., adv.* àmpy
**enter** *v.* mìditra
**entry** *n.* fidìrana
**envelope** *n.* valòpy
**equal** *v.* mitòvy; *n.* fitovìana
**error** *n.* hadisòana
**escape** *v.* mandòsitra; *n.* fandosìrana
**establish** *v.* manòrina
**estimate** *v.* manòmbana; *n.* tombantòmbana

evening *n.* harìva
every *adj.* tsirairày
exact *adj.* màrina
example *n.* òhatra
exceed *v.* mihòatra
except *prep.* àfa-tsy
exchange *v.* manakàlo; *n.* takàlo
exchange rate *n.* sàndam-bòla, cours *fr.*
excursion *n.* fitsangatsangànana
excuse *v.* miàla tsìny; *n.* fialàn-tsìny
expedition *n.* dìa
expense *n.* vòla làny
expensive *adj.* làfo
explain *v.* manazàva
explanation *n.* fanazavàna
extend *v.* manalàva
extension *n.* fanalavàna
eye *n.* màso

# F

fabric *n.* làmba
face *n.* tarèhy
fail *v.* tsy mahòmby
fall *v.* mianjèra; *n.* fianjeràna
false *adj.* dìso
family *n.* fianakavìana
famous *adj.* malàza
far *adj.* làvitra
fare *n.* sàran-dàlana, frais *fr*
farewell *interj.* velòma!
fashion *n.* lamàody
fast *adj.* hàingana
fat *adj.* matàvy
father *n.* rày

**favorite** *adj.* tìana indrìndra
**fear** *v.* matàhotra; *n.* tàhotra
**feature** *n.* tòetra manòkana
**February** *n.* febroàry
**fee** *n.* vòla alòa
**feed** *v.* mamàhana
**feel** *v.* mahatsàpa
**female** *n.* vàvy
**fence** *v.* mamèfy; *n.* fèfy
**ferry** *n.* bàka
**fetch** *v.* màka
**fever** *n.* tàzo
**fiancé** *n.* fòfom-bàdy
**field** *n.* sàha
**fight** *v.* miàdy; *n.* àdy
**fill** *v.* mamèno
**filling** *n.* tsèntsi-nìfy (teeth)
**film** *n.* sary mihètsika
**finance** *v.* miàntoka; *n.* fitantànana vòla
**finances** *n.* toè-bòla
**find** *v.* mahìta
**fine** *adj.* tsàra; *n.* vòla sàzy
**finger** *n.* ràntsana
**finish** *v.* mamìta
**fire** *n.* àfo
**fish** *n.* tròndro
**five** *adj.* dìmy
**fix** *v.* manambòatra
**floor** *n.* goròdona
**flow** *v.* mikorìana
**fly** *v.* manìdina
**fold** *v.* mamòritra
**follow** *v.* manàraka
**fool** *n.* adàla
**for** *prep.* ho an'
**foreigner** *n.* vahìny

**forget** *v.* manadìno
**fork** *n.* forsèty
**form** *n.* bìka
**fortnight** *n.* tàpa-bòlana
**fountain** *n.* loharàno
**four** *adj.* èfatra
**free** *adj.* àfaka
**frequent** *adj.* matètika
**Friday** *n.* zomà
**friend** *n.* nàmana
**frighten** *v.* mampitàhotra
**frog** *n.* sàhona
**from** *prep.* àvy
**fruit** *n.* voankàzo
**full** *adj.* fèno
**funny** *adj.* mahatsikàiky
**furniture** *n.* fànaka

# G

**game** *n.* làlao
**garbage** *n.* fàko
**garden** *n.* zaridàina
**garment** *n.* fitafiana
**gasoline** *n.* lasàntsy
**gentle** *adj.* malèmy fanàhy
**genuine** *adj.* tèna ìzy
**get** *v.* mahàzo
**gift** *n.* fanomèzana
**girl** *n.* zazavàvy
**give** *v.* manomè
**glad** *adj.* fàly
**glasses** *n.* solomàso (eye)
**glue** *n.* lakàoly
**go** *v.* mandèha
**God** *n.* Andriamànitra

**gold** *n., adj.* volamèna
**good** *adj.* tsàra
**good-bye** *interj.* velòma
**goose** *n.* gìsa
**government** *n.* fanjakàna, governemànta *fr*
**grandchild** *n.* zafikèly
**grandfather** *n.* raibè
**grandmother** *n.* renibè
**grant** *n.* fanampìana
**green** *adj.* màitso
**greet** *v.* miarahàba
**greeting** *n.* fiarahabàna
**grocer** *n.* mpivàrotra
**grocery** *n.* fivaròtana
**grow** *v.* mitòmbo
**growth** *n.* fitombòana
**guarantee** *v.* miàntoka; *n.* àntoka
**guest** *n.* vahìny
**guide** *v.* mitàri-dàlana; *n.* mpitàri-dàlana
**guilty** *adj.* mèloka
**gun** *n.* bàsy

# H

**habit** *n.* fahazàrana
**hair** *n.* vòlo
**hairdresser** *n.* mpanào vòlo
**half** *adj.* antsàsany
**ham** *n.* jambon *fr*
**hand** *n.* tànana
**handicapped** *adj.* kilemàina
**handicrafts** *n.* taozàvatra
**handkerchief** *n.* mosàra
**happen** *v.* mitrànga
**happy** *adj.* fàly

harbor *n.* pôro
hat *n.* sàtroka
hate *v.* mankahàla
have *v.* mànana
he *pron.* ìzy
head *n.* lòha
headache *n.* arètin'andòha
health *n.* fahasalamàna
healthy *adj.* salàma
hear *v.* mandrè
heart *n.* fo
heat *n.* hafanàna
heavy *adj.* mavèsatra
hello *interj.* Manahòana!, Akòry! (dial.)
help *v.* manàmpy; *n.* fanampìana
help! *interj.* Vonjèo!
her *pron.* àzy
here *adv.* èto
hide *v.* miàfina
high *adj.* ambòny
him *pron.* àzy
hire *v.* manakaràma
his *pron.* àzy
hit *v.* mandòna
hold *v.* mihàzona
home *n.* fonènana
honey *n.* tantèly
hope *v.* manantèna; *n.* fanantenàna
horrify *v.* mampatàhotra
hospital *n.* hôpitàly
host *n.* tòmpon-tràno
hot *adj.* mafàna
hotel *n.* hôtèly
hour *n.* òra
house *n.* tràno
housekeeper *n.* mpiàsa

**how** *adv.* ahòana
**hungry** *adj.* nòana
**hunt** *v.* mihàza
**hurt** *v.* mandràtra; *adj.* maràtra
**husband** *n.* vàdy


# I

**ice** *n.* glàsy
**ice cream** *n.* glàsy
**idea** *n.* hèvitra
**if** *conj.* ràha
**ill** *adj.* maràry
**illegal** *adj.* tsy ara-dalàna
**imitate** *v.* màka tàhaka
**immigrant** *n.* mpifìndra mònina
**impossible** *adj.* tsy mèty
**improve** *v.* manatsàra
**incident** *n.* zàva-misèho
**income** *n.* vòla mìditra
**indoors** *n.* ào an-tràno
**industry** *n.* ozìnina taozàvatra
**infant** *n.* zazakèly
**infection** *n.* àreti-mifìndra
**inflammation** *n.* fivontòsana
**inform** *v.* milàza
**information** *n.* filazàna
**insect** *n.* bibikèly
**inside** *adv.* ào anàtiny
**instructions** *n.* fepètra
**insurance** *n.* àntoka, assurance *fr*
**interesting** *adj.* mahalìana
**interpret** *v.* mandìka tèny
**introduce** *v.* mampahafàntatra òlona
**iron** *v.* mipàsoka; *n.* fèra

**island** *n.* nòsy
**item** *n.* zàvatra

# J

**jacket** *n.* palitào
**jail** *n.* figadràna
**jam** *n.* confiture *fr*
**January** *n.* janoàry
**jeweler** *n.* mpanào firàvaka, bijoutier *fr*
**jewelry** *n.* firàvaka
**job** *n.* àsa
**joke** *v.* mivazivàzy; *n.* vazivàzy
**journal** *n.* gazèty
**journey** *n.* dìa
**joy** *n.* fifalìana
**judge** *v.* mitsàra; *n.* mpitsàra
**July** *n.* jolày
**jump** *v.* misàoty
**junction** *n.* fihàonan-dàlana
**justification** *n.* fanamarìnana
**justify** *v.* manamàrina

# K

**keep** *v.* mitàna
**key** *n.* lakilè
**kid** *n.* zàza
**kill** *v.* mamòno
**kind** *adj.* tsàra fanàhy; *n.* karàzana
**kiss** *v.* manòroka; *n.* òroka
**kitchen** *n.* lakozìa
**knee** *n.* lohàlika
**knife** *n.* àntsy

**knock** *v.* mandòna
**knot** *v.* mamèhy; *n.* vòna
**know** *v.* mahalàla
**known** *adj.* fàntatra

# L

**label** *n.* màrika
**ladder** *n.* tòhatra
**lady** *n.* vehivàvy
**lake** *n.* farìhy
**lamp** *n.* jìro
**land** *v.* mipètraka; *n.* tàny
**language** *n.* tèny, fitèny
**large** *adj.* lehibè
**last** *adj.* fàrany
**late** *adj.* tàra
**laugh** *v.* mihomèhy; *n.* hèhy
**laundry** *n.* làmba malòto
**law** *n.* lalàna
**lay** *v.* mamètraka
**lead** *v.* mitàrika
**leader** *n.* mpitàrika
**leaf** *n.* ràvina
**learn** *v.* miànatra
**leather** *n.* hòditra
**leave** *v.* miàla, miàinga
**left** *adj.* havìa
**leg** *n.* tòngotra
**legend** *n.* angàno
**leisure** *n.* fialàm-bòly
**lemur** *n.* gìdro
**lend** *v.* mampìndrana
**length** *n.* halàva
**less** *adj.* kelikèly kokòa

**let** v. mamèla
**letter** n. taratàsy
**lettuce** n. salàdy
**license** n. alàlana
**lie** v. mandàinga; n. làinga
**life** n. fiàinana
**lift** v. mibàta
**light** n. jìro; adj. màivana
**like** v. tìa
**lip** n. mòlotra
**liquid** n. ràno
**list** n. lìsitra
**litter** n. lìtatra
**little** adj. kèly
**live** v. mipètraka
**liver** n. àty
**long** adj. làva
**look** v. mijèry (at); mitàdy (for)
**lorry** n. kamiào (truck)
**lose** v. manàry
**lost** adj. vèry
**love** v. tìa; n. fitiàvana
**lovely** adj. tsàra tarèhy
**low** adj. ìva
**luck** n. vìntana
**lunch** n. sakàfo atoàndro

# M

**machine** n. masìnina
**mad** adj. adàla
**madam** n. madàma
**mail** n. taratàsy
**make** v. manào
**malagasy** n., adj. malagàsy, gàsy

**malaria** *n.* tàzo
**male** *n.* làhy
**man** *n.* lehilàhy
**management** *n.* fitondràna
**manager** *n.* mpitòndra
**many** *adj.* màro
**map** *n.* sarintàny
**March** *n.* màrsa
**market** *n.* tsèna
**marriage** *n.* mariàzy
**marry** *v.* manambàdy
**massage** *v.* manòtra; *n.* òtra
**master** *n.* lehibè
**match** *n.* afokàsika; *adj.* mitòvy
**mattress** *n.* kidòro
**may** *v.* mèty manào
**May** *n.* mày
**meal** *n.* sakàfo
**mean** *v.* milàza hèvitra; *adj.* ràtsy fanàhy
**measure** *v.* mandrèfy; *n.* rèfy
**meat** *n.* hèna
**medicine** *n.* fanafòdy
**meet** *v.* mihàona
**meeting** *n.* fihàonana
**member** *n.* mpikàmbana
**merchant** *n.* mpivàrotra
**mess** *n.* koròntana
**message** *n.* hàfatra
**method** *n.* fòmba fiàsa
**midnight** *n.* sasak'àlina
**milk** *n.* ronòno
**mind** *n.* sàina
**mine** *pron.* àhy
**minister** *n.* minìstra
**minute** *n.* minìtra
**mirror** *n.* fitàratra

**Miss** *n.* Ramatoakèly
**miss** *v.* tsy mahatràtra
**mistake** *n.* dìso
**Mister** *n.* Andriamatòa
**mix** *v.* mampifangàro
**modify** *v.* manòva
**Monday** *n.* alatsinàiny
**monkey** *n.* gìdro
**month** *n.* vòlana
**monument** *n.* tsàngam-bàto
**moon** *n.* vòlana
**moonlight** *n.* diavòlana
**more** *adv.* bebe kokòa
**mosquito** *n.* mòka
**mother** *n.* rèny
**mountain** *n.* tèndrombòhitra
**mouth** *n.* vàva
**move** *v.* mihètsika
**mud** *n.* fòtaka
**murder** *v.* mamòno òlona
**murderer** *n.* mpamòno òlona
**museum** *n.* musée *fr*
**mushroom** *n.* hòlatra
**music** *n.* mozìka
**musician** *n.* mpitèndry zàva-manèno

# N

**name** *n.* anàrana
**nap** *n.* tòrimaso kèly
**nation** *n.* firenèna
**nationality** *n.* fihavìana
**nature** *n.* zàva-manan'àina
**near** *prep.* akàiky
**necessary** *adj.* ilàina

**neck** *n.* tènda
**need** *v.* mìla
**negotiate** *v.* mifampiraharàha
**neighbor** *n.* mpifanòlo-bodirìndrina
**never** *adv.* na ovìana na ovìana
**new** *adj.* vaovào
**newspaper** *n.* gazèty
**next** *adj., adv.* manàraka
**nice** *adj.* tsàra
**night** *n.* àlina
**nine** *adj.* sìvy
**no** *adv.* tsìa
**noisy** *adj.* mankadìlo
**nonsense** *n.* tsy mìsy dìkany
**north** *adv.* avàratra
**nose** *n.* òrona
**November** *n.* novàmbra
**now** *adv.* izào
**number** *n.* ìsa
**nun** *n.* masèra
**nurse** *n.* infirmière *fr*

# O

**object** *n.* zàvatra (thing); *n.* tànjona (aim)
**observe** *v.* mandìnika
**obtain** *v.* mahàzo
**occupation** *n.* àsa
**occur** *v.* mitrànga
**o'clock** *adv.* òra
**October** *n.* ôktôbra
**offer** *v.* manòlotra
**office** *n.* birào
**often** *adv.* matètika
**oil** *n.* solitàny

okay *adj.* ekèna
on *prep.* ambòny
one *adj.* iràt
onion *n.* tongòlo
only *adv.* fòtsiny
open *v.* manòkatra; *adj.* misòkatra
operate *v.* mampandèha
operation *n.* fandidìana (chirurgical)
opinion *n.* hèvitra
opposite *adj.* mifanòhitra
or *conj.* na
orange *n.* voasàry (fruit)
order *v.* mandìdy (to command); manàfatra
   (restaurant); *n.* dìdy (a command; a cut)
organization *n.* fikambànana
other *adj., adv.* hàfa
our *pron.* anày (excl.); antsìka (incl.)
out *adv.* ào ivèlany
outside *adv.* èny ivèlany
owner *n.* tòmpony

# P

pack *v.* mampìrin' èntana
package *n.* fonòsan'èntana
page *n.* pèjy (of a book)
pain *n.* fanaintàinana
painful *adj.* maràry
paint *v.* mandòko; *n.* lòko
pal *n.* sakàiza
palace *n.* làpa
pale *adj.* hàtsatra
paper *n.* taratàsy
pardon *n.* azafàdy
parents *n.* rày aman-drèny

**park** *n.* zaridàina
**part** *v.* mizàra; *n.* ampàhany
**participate** *v.* mandrày anjàra
**passenger** *n.* mpandèha
**path** *n.* làlan-kèly
**pay** *v.* mandòa vòla
**payment** *n.* fandoàvam-bòla
**peach** *n.* pàiso
**pen** *n.* pènina
**pencil** *n.* pensìly
**people** *n.* vahòaka
**pepper** *n.* dipoàvatra
**perfect** *adj.* tònga làfatra
**perhaps** *adv.* angàmba
**period** *n.* fotòana voafètra (of time)
**permission** *n.* fanomèzana alàlana
**permit** *v.* manomè alàlana; *n.* fanomèzan-dàlana
**person** *n.* òlona
**pharmacy** *n.* pharmacie *fr*, farmasìa
**phone** *v.* miàntso telefàonina
**photo** *n.* sàry
**photographer** *n.* mpàka sàry
**physician** *n.* dokotèra
**pick** *v.* mifìdy
**picnic** *n.* fitsangatsangànana
**picture** *n.* sàry
**piece** *n.* pòtiny kèly
**pig** *n.* kisòa
**pill** *n.* fanafòdy
**pillow** *n.* òndana
**pilot** *n.* mpanamòry fiaramanìdina
**pineapple** *n.* mananàsy
**place** *v.* mamètraka; *n.* toèrana
**plague** *n.* pèsta
**plan** *n.* fikasàna
**plane** *n.* fiaramanìdina

plant *v.* mambòly; *n.* zava-manìry
plate *n.* vilìa
play *v.* milalào
player *n.* mpilalào
plea *n.* fialàn-tsìny
pleasant *adj.* mahafinàritra
pleased *adj.* fàly
pleasure *n.* hafalìana
plenty *adj.* bètsaka
plum *n.* pàiso
pocket *n.* pàosy
poison *v.* manapòizina; *n.* pòizina
polite *adj.* mahalàla fòmba
politician *n.* mpanào politìka
poor *adj.* mahàntra
population *n.* mpònina
possess *v.* mànana
possible *adj.* mèty
post *v.* mandèfa taratàsy
postage *n.* sàrany
post office *n.* pàositra
postpone *v.* mampihèmotra
pour *v.* manìdina
poverty *n.* fahantràna
power *n.* hèry
precious *adj.* sàro-bìdy
prefer *v.* tìana kokòa
prepare *v.* manòmana
present *v.* mampisèho; *n.* fanomèzana
president *n.* prezidà
press *v.* manìndry
pretty *adj.* tsàra tarèhy
price *n.* vìdiny
principle *n.* fitsìpika
prison *n.* trànomàizina
private *adj.* privé *fr*

privilege *n.* tòmbon-tsòa
prize *n.* lòka
produce *v.* mamòkatra
product *n.* vòkatra
profession *n.* àsa
progress *v.* mandròso; *n.* fandrosòana
prohibit *v.* mandràra
project *n.* fikasàna
promise *v.* manomè tòky; *n.* fanomèzan-tòky
proof *n.* poròfo
property *n.* fanànana
proposal *n.* hèvitra aròso
protect *v.* miàro
protest *v.* manòhitra
prove *v.* manaporòfo
pull *v.* misìntona
punish *v.* manasàzy
pure *adj.* tsy mìsy fangàrony
purse *n.* pôkètra
put *v.* mamètraka

# Q

quality *n.* tòetra manòkana
quantity *n.* habetsàhana
quarrel *n.* àdi-hèvitra; *v.* miàdy hèvitra
question *n.* fanontanìana; *v.* manontàny
quick *adj.* hàingana
quiet *adj., adv.* mangìna
quit *v.* mitsàhatra

# R

rabbit *n.* bìtro
radio *n.* radiô

**rain** *v.* manòrana; *n.* òrana
**rat** *n.* voalàvo
**reach** *v.* mahatràtra
**read** *v.* mamàky
**ready** *adj.* vònona
**real** *adj.* màrina
**realization** *n.* fanatanteràhana
**realize** *v.* manantantèraka
**reason** *n.* àntony
**receipt** *n.* rosìa
**receive** *v.* mandrày
**red** *adj.* mèna
**reduce** *v.* mampihèna
**refrigerator** *n.* frizidèra
**refuge** *n.* fialòfana
**refusal** *n.* fandàvana
**refuse** *v.* mandà
**regular** *adj.* àra-dalàna
**relationship** *n.* fifandràisana
**reliable** *adj.* atokìsana
**religion** *n.* fivavàhana
**remember** *v.* mitadìdy
**remind** *v.* mampatsiàro
**rent** *v.* manòfa; *n.* hòfan-tràno
**repair** *v.* manambòatra
**repeat** *v.* mamèrina
**replace** *v.* manòlo
**request** *v.* mangàtaka; *n.* fangatàhana
**require** *v.* mitàdy
**rescue** *v.* mamònjy
**reservation** *n.* famandrìhana toèrana
**respect** *v.* manàja
**responsible** *adj.* tòmpon'andràikitra
**rest** *v.* miàla sàsatra
**restaurant** *n.* restaurant *fr*
**return** *v.* mivèrina

**reward** *n.* valisòa
**rice** *n.* vàry
**rich** *adj.* manàn-karèna
**right** *adj.* màrina (correct); ankavànana (direction)
**ring** *n.* pèratra
**rinse** *v.* manakòbana
**ripe** *adj.* màsaka
**river** *n.* reniràno
**road** *n.* làlana
**rob** *v.* mandròba
**robber** *n.* jiolàhy
**rock** *n.* vatolàmpy
**roof** *n.* tàfo
**room** *n.* èfitra
**rose** *n.* ràozy
**rotten** *adj.* lo
**round** *adj.* boribòry
**rubbish** *n.* fàko (garbage)
**rule** *n.* fitsìpika
**run** *v.* mihazakàzaka
**rural** *adj.* ambanivòhitra

# S

**sack** *n.* kitàpo
**sad** *adj.* malahèlo
**safe** *adj.* atokìsana
**salad** *n.* salàdy
**salary** *n.* karàma
**salt** *n.* sìra
**Saturday** *n.* asabòtsy
**sauce** *n.* sàosy
**saucepan** *n.* vilàny
**save** *v.* mamònjy
**say** *v.* mitèny

**school** *n.* fianàrana
**scissors** *n.* hèty
**scratch** *v.* mandràngotra; *n.* ràngotra
**sea** *n.* ranomàsina
**seafood** *n.* hàzan-dràno
**search** *v.* mitàdy
**seashore** *n.* mòron-drànomàsina
**season** *n.* fizaràn-tàona
**secret** *n.* tsiambàratèlo
**see** *v.* mahìta
**send** *v.* mandèfa
**service** *n.* àsa àman-draharàha
**seven** *adj.* fìto
**share** *v.* mizàra; *n.* anjàra
**shark** *n.* antsàntsa
**sharp** *adj.* marànitra
**she** *pron.* ìzy
**sheep** *n.* òndry
**sheet** *n.* làmbam-pandrìana (bed linen); taratàsy
(sheet of paper)
**ship** *n.* sàmbo
**shirt** *n.* lòbaka
**shoe** *n.* kiràro
**shoemaker** *n.* mpanào kiràro
**shop** *v.* miantsèna; *n.* fivaròtana
**short** *adj.* fòhy
**shoulder** *n.* sòroka
**shout** *v.* miàntso màfy
**show** *v.* mampisèho; *n.* fampisehòana
**shower** *n.* fandròana
**shut** *v.* manakàtona; *adj.* mikàtona
**sick** *adj.* maràry
**sickness** *n.* arètina
**side** *n.* làfiny irày
**sign** *v.* manào sonìa
**signal** *n.* famantàrana

**signature** *n.* sonìa
**silence** *n.* fahangìnana
**silk** *n.* làndy
**silly** *adj.* dòndrona
**silver** *adj.* volafòtsy
**simple** *adj.* tsòtra
**since** *prep.* hatràmin'ny
**sing** *v.* mihìra
**single** *adj.* tsy manambàdy
**sink** *v.* milèntika; *n.* fanasàna vilìa
**Sir** *n.* tòmpokolàhy
**sister** *n.* rahavàvy (of a woman); anabàvy (of
    a man)
**sit** *v.* mipètraka
**six** *adj.* ènina
**size** *n.* habè
**skin** *n.* hòditra
**skirt** *n.* zìpo
**sky** *n.* lànitra
**sleep** *v.* matòry
**small** *adj.* kèly
**smell** *v.* mamòfona; *n.* fòfona
**smile** *v.* mitsìky; *n.* tsìky
**smoke** *v.* manètroka; *n.* sètroka
**snail** *n.* sìfotra
**snake** *n.* bibilàva
**snakebite** *n.* kàikitra bibilàva
**soap** *n.* savòny
**social** *adj.* mòmba ny fiaràha-monina
**society** *n.* fikambànana
**sock** *n.* ba kiràro
**sofa** *n.* sèza làva
**soldier** *n.* miaramìla
**something** *n.* zàvatra
**son** *n.* zànaka làhy
**song** *n.* hìra

sore *adj.* manetsètra
sorry *adj.* manènina
soup *n.* lasòpy
sound *n.* feo; *adj.* salàma
south *adj.* atsìmo
speak *v.* mitèny
spend *v.* mandàny
spider *n.* àla
sport *n.* fanàtanjahan-tena
spring *n.* lohatàona (season)
stairs *n.* tòhatra
stamp *n.* tàmbra, hajìa
stand *v.* mijòro
star *n.* kìntana
start *v.* manòmboka; *n.* fanombòhana
statue *n.* sàry sìkotra
stay *v.* mipètraka
steak *n.* hèna endàsina, biftèka
steal *v.* mangàlatra
step *n.* dìngana
sticky *adj.* madìty
still *v.* mampitòny; *adj.* tsy mihètsika
stocks *n.* pètra-bòla (bonds and other commercial
    papers)
stomach *n.* vavòny
stone *n.* vàto
stop *v.* mijànona; *n.* fijanònana
storm *n.* tafìo-drìvotra
straight *adj.* mahìtsy
strange *adj.* hafahàfa
stranger *n.* vahìny
stream *n.* reniràno
street *n.* arabe
strength *n.* hèry
student *n.* mpiànatra
study *v.* miànatra

**stuff** *n.* zàvatra
**succeed** *v.* mahòmby
**sudden** *adj.* tàmpoka
**suffer** *v.* mijàly
**sufficient** *adj.* àmpy
**sugar** *n.* siramàmy
**suit** *n.* complet *fr*
**suitcase** *n.* valìzy
**sum** *n.* totàly
**summer** *n.* fahavàratra
**summon** *v.* miàntso
**sun** *n.* masoàndro
**Sunday** *n.* alahàdy
**sunshine** *n.* fahazavàn'ny masoàndro
**supper** *n.* sakàfo harìva
**support** *v.* manòhana
**sure** *adj.* matòky
**surname** *n.* anàrana
**surprise** *v.* manàmpoka
**swallow** *v.* mitèlina
**sweep** *v.* mamàfa
**sweet** *adj.* màmy
**sweetheart** *n.* malàla
**swim** *v.* milomàno
**swollen** *adj.* mivònto


# T

**table** *n.* latàbatra
**tablespoon** *n.* sòtro lehibè
**taboo** *n.* fàdy
**tailor** *n.* mpanjàitra, couturier *fr*
**take** *v.* màka
**talk** *v.* mitèny
**tall** *adj.* làva

**task** *n.* àsa
**taste** *v.* manàndrana; *n.* tsìro
**taxi** *n.* taxi
**tea** *n.* ditè
**teach** *v.* mampiànatra
**teacher** *n.* mpampiànatra
**tear** *v.* mandròvitra
**technique** *n.* teknìka
**telegram** *n.* telegràma
**telephone** *v.* miàntso telefàonina; *n.* telefàonina
**television** *n.* fahìtalàvitra
**tell** *v.* milàza
**temperature** *n.* hafanàna
**terrible** *adj.* mahatsiràvina
**test** *v.* manàndrana; *n.* àndrana
**thank** *v.* misàotra
**theft** *n.* hàlatra
**their** *pron.* àzy
**them** *pron.* àzy irèo
**there** *adv.* èny (visible), àny (invisible)
**these** *pron.* irèto
**they** *pron.* ìzy irèo
**thief** *n.* mpangàlatra
**thing** *n.* zàvatra
**think** *v.* mihèvitra
**thirsty** *adj.* mangetahèta
**this** *pron.* ity
**those** *pron.* irèo
**threaten** *v.* mampitàhotra
**three** *adj.* tèlo
**throat** *n.* tènda
**throw** *v.* manìpy
**thunder** *v.* mikòtroka; *n.* kòtroka
**Thursday** *n.* alakamìsy
**ticket** *n.* biè
**tie** *n.* kravàto; *v.* mamàtotra

**time** *n.* fotòana
**tired** *adj.* vìzaka
**to** *prep.* mankàny
**today** *adv., n.* anìo
**together** *adv.* miàraka
**toilet** *n.* tràno fivoàhana, toilettes *fr*
**tomato** *n.* voatabìa
**tomorrow** *adv.* rahampìtso
**tongue** *n.* lèla
**tonight** *adv., n.* anìo àlina
**too** *adv.* kòa
**tooth** *n.* nìfy
**tortoise** *n.* sòkatra
**total** *adj.* totàly
**touch** *v.* mikàsika
**tour** *n.* fizahàn-tàny
**tourist** *n.* mpizàha tàny
**tow** *v.* mitàrika
**town** *n.* tanàna
**trade** *v.* manào vàrotra fifanankalòzana; *n.* vàrotra
  fifanankalòzana
**traffic** *n.* fifamoivoìzana
**train** *n.* masìnina
**translate** *v.* mandìka tèny
**transport** *v.* mitàtitra; *n.* fitatèrana
**tree** *n.* hàzo
**trick** *v.* mamìtaka; *n.* fìtaka
**truck** *n.* kamiào
**truth** *n.* ny màrina
**try** *v.* manàndrana
**Tuesday** *n.* talàta
**tunnel** *n.* tonèlina
**turn** *v.* miòdina
**twilight** *n.* mazàva ràtsy
**two** *adj.* ròa
**type** *n.* karàzana

# U

**umbrella** *n.* èlo
**unable** *adj.* tsy àfaka
**uncle** *n.* dadatòa
**unconscious** *adj.* tsy mahatsiàro tèna
**under** *prep.* ambàny
**understand** *v.* mahàzo
**underwear** *n.* fitafiana anàtiny
**unexpected** *adj.* tàmpoka
**unfair** *adj.* tsy ràriny
**university** *n.* oniversitè
**unknown** *adj.* tsy fàntatra
**unless** *conj.* ràha tsy hoè
**unlimited** *adj.* tsy voafètra
**until** *prep.* mandrapaha-
**unwilling** *adj.* malàina
**up** *adv.* miàkatra; *adj.* ambòny
**upon** *prep.* èo ambòny
**upstairs** *n.* ambòny rìhina
**urgent** *adj.* màika
**us** *pron.* anày (excl.); antsìka (incl.)
**use** *v.* mampiàsa; *n.* fampiasàna
**useful** *adj.* àzo ampiasàina
**usual** *adj.* fanào
**usually** *adj.* mazàna

# V

**vacation** *n.* fakàn-drìvotra
**valid** *adj.* mànan-kèry
**valley** *n.* lohasàha
**value** *n.* vìdy
**vanilla** *n.* lavanìla
**various** *adj.* sàmy hàfa

**vary** *v.* miovaòva
**vase** *n.* vàzy
**vegetable** *n.* ànana, légumes *fr*
**vegetation** *n.* zàva-manìry
**vehicle** *n.* fiàra
**very** *adj.* tokòa
**via** *prep.* mandàlo àny
**visit** *v.* mamàngy; *n.* famangìana
**voice** *n.* fèo
**vote** *v.* mandàtsa-bàto; *n.* fifidiànana
**voyage** *n.* fandehànana

# W

**wages** *n.* karàma
**waist** *n.* valàhana
**wait** *v.* miàndry; *n.* fiandràsana
**wake** *v.* mamòha
**walk** *v.* mandèha an-tòngotra; *n.* fandehànana
**wall** *n.* rìndrina
**wallet** *n.* pokètra kèly
**want** *v.* mìla
**war** *n.* àdy
**wardrobe** *n.* lalimoàra
**warehouse** *n.* magazày
**warm** *v.* mamàna; *adj.* mafàna
**warn** *v.* mampitàndrina
**wash** *v.* manàsa (sth); misàsa (oneself)
**wasp** *n.* fanènitra
**watch** *v.* mijèry; *n.* famantaranàndro
**water** *n.* ràno
**wave** *v.* mikopakòpaka (one's hand); *n.* ònja
(water)
**way** *n.* làlana
**weak** *adj.* malèmy

**wear** *v.* mitàfy
**weather** *n.* toetr'àndro
**wed** *v.* mampàka-bàdy
**wedding** *n.* mariàzy
**Wednesday** *n.* alarobìa
**week** *n.* herinàndro
**weekly** *adv.* ìsan-kerinàndro
**weigh** *v.* mandànja
**weight** *n.* lànja
**weird** *adj.* hafahàfa
**welcome!** *interj.* tònga soa!
**well** *adj., adv.* tsàra
**wet** *adj.* lèna
**wheat** *n.* vàrim-bazàha
**when** *adv.* rehèfa
**where** *adv.* àiza
**while** *conj.* ràha
**white** *adj.* fòtsy
**why** *adv.* nahòana
**wife** *n.* vàdy
**wild** *adj.* dìa
**willing** *adj.* vònona
**wind** *n.* rìvotra
**window** *n.* varavarankèly
**windy** *adj.* mandrìvotra
**wine** *n.* divày
**wish** *v.* manìry; *n.* fanirìana
**with** *prep.* miàraka àmin'
**without** *prep.* tsy mìsy
**witness** *n.* vavòlombèlona
**woman** *n.* vehivàvy
**wonderful** *adj.* mahafinàritra
**word** *n.* tèny
**work** *v.* miàsa; *n.* àsa
**world** *n.* izào tontòlo izào
**worm** *n.* kànkana
**worry** *v.* miahiàhy; *n.* ahiàhy

**wound** *v.* mandràtra; *n.* ràtra
**write** *v.* manòratra
**wrong** *adj.* dìso


# Y

**year** *n.* tàona
**yearly** *adv.* ìsan-tàona
**yellow** *adj.* màvo
**yes** *adv.* èny
**yesterday** *adv.* omàly
**yet** *conj.* kanèfa; *adv.* hatràmin'izào
**yoghurt** *n.* iaòrta
**you** *pron.* ianào (sing.); ianarèo (pl.)
**young** *adj.* tanòra
**your** *adj.* anào (sing.); anarèo (pl.)
**youth** *n.* fahatanoràna
**yummy** *adj.* matsìro


# Z

**zeal** *n.* fahazotòana
**zero** *n.* àotra
**zone** *n.* faritàny
**zoo** *n.* zoo *fr*

# MALAGASY PHRASEBOOK

| | |
|---|---|
| BASIC WORDS AND PHRASES | 96 |
| MEETING AND GREETING | 98 |
| FOOD AND DRINK | 105 |
| ACCOMMODATIONS | 111 |
| TRAVEL | 116 |
| TRIPS AND SIGHTSEEING | 121 |
| DIRECTIONS | 126 |
| COMMUNICATIONS | 128 |
| SHOPPING | 131 |
| MONEY | 135 |
| HEALTH | 137 |
| ADMINISTRATION | 143 |
| WEATHER | 146 |
| NATURE | 148 |
| POLITICS | 153 |
| EMERGENCIES | 155 |
| LOSS AND ROBBERY | 158 |
| NUMBERS | 160 |
| TIME | 163 |
| WEIGHTS AND MEASURES | 166 |
| COLORS | 167 |
| FACTS ON MADAGASCAR | 169 |
| MAP OF MADAGASCAR AND MAYOTTE | 171 |

# BASIC WORDS AND PHRASES

## ◆ Basic Words and Phrases

Malagasy speakers generally greet each other with:

**Manahòana!**, **Manakòry**, or **Akòry!** All three expressions mean: Hello! or How are you? or Good morning/Good afternoon/Good evening.

Fine, thank you.
  **Tsàra fa misàotra.**
Good-bye!
  **Velòma!**
Please
  **Azafàdy**
Thank you.
  **Misàotra.**
You're welcome.
  **Tsy mìsy fisàorana.**
Excuse me!
  **Azafàdy kèly e!**
Help! **Vonjèo!**
Could you help me please?
  **Àfaka manàmpy àhy ve ianào?**
Do you speak English?
  **Mitèny anglìsy ve ianào?**
I do not speak Malagasy.
  **Tsy mahày mitèny gàsy àho.**
I need ... .
  **Mìla ... àho.**
I am sorry.
  **Miàla tsìny àho.**
Yes
  **Èny**
No
  **Tsìa**

Watch out!

**Tandrèmo!**

Where is the ... ?

**Àiza ny ... ?**

Can you show me the way to ... ?

**Àiza ny làlana mankàny ... ?**

Can you drive me to ... ?

**Àfaka manàtitra àhy àny ... ve ianào?**

## ◆ Meeting and Greeting

### *Terms of Address*

Malagasy are quite aware of status. Therefore, when addressing an unknown person or a respectable person of either sex, one uses the address form **tòmpoko**, 'my Lord'. This applies to polite questions, requests, answers, comments and simple statements. When you greet someone you do not know, when you speak to someone who is older than you, or when you are in an office or business setting, it is polite to finish your greetings, questions and answers with the conventional address form **tòmpoko**.

Can you help me?
    **Àfaka manàmpy àhy ve ianào?** (neutral form)
    **Àfaka manàmpy àhy ve ianào, tòmpoko?**
      (polite form)

It is very far from here.
    **Làvitra be èto ìo.** (neutral form)
    **Làvitra be èto ìo, tòmpoko.** (polite form)

When you are asked something and would like to answer yes or no, the polite forms are:

Yes
    **Èny, tòmpoko.**
No
    **Tsìa, tòmpoko.**

Miss **Ramatòakèly**
Mr. **Andriamatòa, Ramosè** (optionally)
Mrs. **Ramatòa**
polite address form **tòmpoko**
sir and madam **tòmpokolàhy sy tòmpokovàvy**

## Introductions

What is your name?
**Ìza no anaranào?**
My name is ... .
**... no anàrako.**
This is ... .
**Ity ... .**
my colleague
**ny mpiàra-miàsa àmiko**
my/your relative
**ny hàvako/ny havanào**
my/your friend
**ny nàmako/ny namanào**
my/your family
**ny fianakavìako/ny fianakavìanào**
my/your husband/wife
**ny vàdiko/ny vàdinào**
my/your children
**ny zànako/ny zanakào**
my/your daughter
**ny zànako vàvy/ny zànakào vàvy**
my/your son
**ny zànako làhy/ny zanakào làhy**
my/your parents
**ny rày àman-drèniko/ny rày àman-drèninào**
my/your mother
**ny rèniko/ny rèninào**
my/your father
**ny ràiko/ny rainào**
my/your grandparents
**ny ràibe sy rènibeko/ny ràibe sy rènibenào**
my/your uncle
**ny dadatòako/ny dadatòanào**
my/your aunt
**ny nenitòako/ny nenitòanào**

my / your brother
**ny rahalàhiko/ny rahalàhinào** (the brother of a man)
**ny anadàhiko/ny anadàhinào** (the brother of a woman)
my/your sister
**ny rahavàviko/ny rahavàvinào** (the sister of a woman)
**ny anabàviko/ny anabàvinào** (the sister of a man)
my/your cousin
**ny cousin-ako/ny cousin-anào** (male)
**ny cousine-ako/ny cousine-anào** (female)
my/your grandson/granddaughter
**ny zàfikèliko/ny zàfikèlinào**
my/your parents-in-law
**ny rafòzako/ny rafòzanào**

| What do you do? | **Ìnona no asanào?** |
|---|---|
| I am a/an … . | **… àho.** |
| administrator | **administratèra** |
| architect | **arsitèkta** |
| business person | **mpanào afèra** |
| carpenter | **mpandràfitra** |
| dentist | **mpanào nìfy** |
| diplomat | **diplômàty** |
| doctor | **dokotèra** |
| engineer | **injenièra** |
| journalist | **mpanào gazèty** |
| judge | **mpitsàra** |
| manual worker | **mpanào àsa tànana** |
| mechanic | **mécanicien** *fr* |
| nurse | **infirmier** *fr* |
| office worker | **mpiàsa birào** |
| pilot | **mpanamòry fiaramanìdina** |
| scientist | **mpikàroka** |

| | |
|---|---|
| secretary | **sekretèra** |
| soldier | **miaramìla** |
| student | **mpiànatra** |
| surgeon | **mpandìdy** |
| teacher | **mpampiànatra** |

| | |
|---|---|
| How old are you? | **Fìry tàona ianào?** |
| I am ... years old. | **... tàona àho.** |

| | |
|---|---|
| Where are you from? | **Àvy àiza ianào?** |
| Where do you live? | **Àiza ianào no mipètraka?** |
| I am from ... | **Avy àny ... àho.** |
| I live in ... | **Àny ... àho no mipètraka.** |
|     Australia | **Aostralìa** |
|     Austria | **Aotrìsy** |
|     England | **Angletèra** |
|     Germany | **Alemàina** |
|     Madagascar | **Madagasikàra** |
|     Switzerland | **Soìsy** |
|     the United States | **Amerìka** |

(The names of the English-speaking African countries are the same as in English.)

| | |
|---|---|
| Are you married? | **Manambàdy ve ianào?** |
| I am ... . | **... àho.** |
|     single | **tsy mbòla manambàdy** |
|     married | **manambàdy** |
|     divorced | **nisàraka** |
|     widowed | **màty vàdy** |
| I have a child. | **Mànan-jànaka àho.** |

Do you speak English/Malagasy?
**Mitèny anglìsy/gàsy ve ianào?**
I do not speak English/Malagasy.
**Tsy mahày mitèny anglìsy/gàsy àho.**

Yes, I do.
**Ie, mitèny anglìsy àho.**

No, I don't.
**Tsy mitèny anglìsy àho.**

I understand a little.
**Mahàzo kèly àho.**

Nice to meet you.
**Fàly mahalàla anào.**


## Greetings and Leave-takings

How are you? or Hello! or Good morning!/Good
afternoon!/Good evening!
**Manahòana?** or **Akòry?**

Fine, thanks.
**Tsàra fa misàotra.**

Good night!
**Tafandrìa màndry!**

Good-bye!
**Velòma!**

See you!
**Màndra-pihàona!**

Bon voyage! (good journey)
**Soàva dìa!**

Bon appétit! (eat well)
**Mazotòa hòmana!**

Welcome!
**Tònga sòa!**

Merry Christmas!
**Tràtry ny Krismàsy!**

Happy New Year!
**Tràtry ny tàona!**

Happy birthday!
**Bon anniversaire!** *fr*

Congratulations!
**Arahabàina!**

Polite forms of greetings and leave-takings are accompanied by the address form **tòmpoko**:

Good morning/good afternoon/good evening/
    how are you?
    **Manahòana, tòmpoko?**
Good-bye!
    **Velòma, tòmpoko.**
See you!
    **Màndra-pihàona, tòmpoko.**

Numerous leave-taking forms are available for Malagasy speakers depending on the circumstances. In informal short casual encounters on the street, speakers may say: **Ndào àry alòa e!** 'Let us go first!'

The answer to this leave-taking routine is the same:
**Ndào àry alòa e!**

Very often Malagasy speakers add this leave-taking form:

**Mampamàngy àny àmin'ny ankìzy e!** Literally: Greet the children! or **Màndra-pihàona!** See you!

Short casual encounters on the street generally call for the following typical routine greeting and leave-taking sequence:

— **Manahòana?**
    How are you?
— **Tsàra fa misàotra. Manahòana ianarèo?**
    Fine, thanks. How are you (you and your family)?
— **Tsàra fa misàotra.** Fine, thanks.

— **Ndào àry alòa fa mampamàngy àny àmin'ny
    ankìzy e!**

Let us go first! Greet the children!

— **Misàotra. Ndào àry fa velòma!**

Thanks. So let us go. Good-bye!

— **Màndra-pihàona!**

See you!

## ◆ Food and Drink

*Vary* or rice is the main element of any Malagasy meal: Malagasy people eat rice three times a day. Rice is usually eaten with a garnish made of vegetables, fish, meat or soup.

Typical Malagasy dishes are **romàzava** (beef and vegetable stew or vegetable stew only) and **ravitòto** (pork stew with manioc greens). Rice dishes are often accompanied by **lasàry**, a hot, pickled vegetable curry (mainly cabbage and carrots) or by **sakày**, a very hot mashed mixture of piment and ginger.

The available range of tropical fruits in markets is very tempting. Because of possible stomach irritation and its consequences (like diarrhea) you should avoid trying different sorts at once (coconuts, pineapples, lychees, mangoes).

Before starting to eat, Malagasy speakers usually say: **Mazotòa hòmana!** Enjoy your meal!

Do you know a good restaurant?
    **Mahafàntatra restaurant tsàra ve ianào?**
I would like a table, please.
    **Latàbatra irày, azafàdy.**
The menu, please.
    **Kàrta, azafàdy.**
I would like to order.
    **Sàika hanào kômàndy àho.**
Do you have ... ?
    **Mìsy ... ve?**
We don't have ... .
    **Tsy mànana ... izahày.**

# FOOD AND DRINK

I/we am/are thirsty.
> **Mangetahèta àho/izahày.**

I/we am/are hungry.
> **Nòana àho/izahày.**

I am a vegetarian/I do not eat meat.
> **Tsy òman-kèna àho.**

Can I order some more ... ?
> **Àfaka mbòla mikômàndy ... àho ve?**

I have not ordered this.
> **Tsy nanàfatra an'ity àho.**

What is this?
> **Ìnona ity?**

That's all. Thank you.
> **Izày fa misàotra.**

It was delicious.
> **Natsìro be.**

I want to eat more.
> **Mbòla te-hihìnana àho.**

I have finished eating.
> **Vìta sakàfo àho.**

I am full.
> **Vòky àho.**

The bill, please.
> **Ny addition, azafàdy.**

Can you give me a receipt?
> **Àzonào omèna reçu àho ve?**

Where are the toilets?
> **Àiza ny tràno fivoàhana?**

## WORDS

| | |
|---|---|
| an ashtray | **cendrier** *fr* |
| a glass | **vèra** |
| a glass of water | **ràno irày vèra** |

| | |
|---|---|
| a glass of beer | **labièra irày vèra** |
| a bottle | **tavoahàngy** |
| a bottle of water | **ràno àmin'ny tavoahàngy** |
| a bottle of beer | **labièra irày tavoahàngy** |
| another bottle | **tavoahàngy irày** |
| a bottle opener | **fanokàfana tavoahàngy** |
| a corkscrew | **tire-bouchon** *fr* |
| a bottle of red wine | **divày mèna irày tavoahàngy** |
| a bottle of white wine | **divày fòtsy irày tavoahàngy** |
| a cup | **kàopy** |
| a cup of tea | **dité irày kàopy** |
| a cup of coffee | **kafè irày kàopy** |
| an order | **kômàndy** |
| the bill | **addition** *fr* |
| the receipt | **reçu** *fr* |
| salt | **sìra** |
| sugar | **siramàmy** |
| pepper | **poàvra** |
| bad | **ràtsy** |
| bad-tasting | **ràtsy tsìro** |
| bitter | **mangìdy** |
| cold | **mangatsìaka** |
| delicious | **matsìro** |
| good | **tsàra** |
| hot | **mamày** |
| ripe | **màsaka** |
| salty | **be sìra** |
| sour | **marikìvy** |
| spicy | **masìaka** |
| sweet | **màmy** |
| tasteless | **matsàtso** |
| to order | **manàfatra** |
| unripe | **mànta** |

# FOOD AND DRINK

## Breakfast

At breakfast, Malagasy generally eat rice cooked with water, called **vàry sosòa.** You may also have the traditional **vàry amin'ànana** consisting of rice cooked with green vegetables, ginger and tiny red shrimps. Fried smoked beef, **kitòza** is usually served with both dishes.

In hotels and big restaurants, you can have the "European full breakfast" consisting of croissants or baguettes with butter and jam, and coffee or tea.

| | |
|---|---|
| bread | **mòfo** |
| butter | **dibèra** |
| croissant | **croissant** *fr* |
| jam | **confiture** *fr* |

## Lunch and Dinner

The following garnishes are eaten with rice or French fries.

| | |
|---|---|
| beans | **tsaramàso** |
| beef | **hen'òmby** |
| cabbage | **làisòa** |
| crab | **crabe** *fr* |
| dessert | **desèra** |
| dinner | **sakàfo harìva** |
| duck | **gàna** |
| fish | **tròndro** |
| French fries | **òvy endàsina, frites** *fr* |
| fruit | **voankàzo** |
| goose | **gìsa** |
| ground meat | **tòto-kèna** |

| | |
|---|---|
| lobster | **homard** *fr* |
| lunch | **sakàfo atoàndro** |
| meat | **hèna** (any type of meat) |
| noodles | **pàty** |
| oyster | **huître** *fr* |
| pepperoni | **sakày** |
| pork | **hèna kisòa** |
| potato | **òvy** |
| poultry | **vòrona** |
| rice | **vàry** |
| salad | **salàdy** |
| sauce | **sàosy** |
| sausage | **saosìsy** |
| seafood | **hàzan-dràno** |
| soup | **lasòpy** |
| steak | **biftèka** |
| turkey | **vorontsilòza** |
| vegetable | **légumes** *fr* |
| vegetable soup | **lasòpy légumes** |

## *Drinks*

| | |
|---|---|
| water | **ràno** |
| mineral water | **eau minérale** *fr* |
| milk | **ronòno** |
| coffee | **kafè** |
| tea | **ditè** |
| with milk | **sy ronòno** |
| with sugar | **sy siramàmy** |
| hot chocolate | **kakaô** |
| fruit juice | **jus de fruits** *fr*, **rànom-boankàzo** |
| apple juice | **jus de pomme** *fr* |
| orange juice | **rànom-boasàry, jus d'orange** *fr* |

# FOOD AND DRINK

| | |
|---|---|
| pineapple juice | **jus d'ananas** *fr* |
| lemonade | **limonade** *fr* |
| tomato juice | **jus de tomate** *fr* |
| coke | **coca** |
| aperitif | **apéritif** *fr* |
| beer | **labièra** |
| champagne | **champagne** *fr* |
| cognac | **cogniac** *fr* |
| liqueur | **liqueur** *fr* |
| rum | **ràoma** |
| whisky | **whisky** |
| wine | **divày** |
| white wine | **divày fòtsy** |
| red wine | **divày mèna** |

## *Cutlery*

| | |
|---|---|
| bowl | **bàola** |
| can | **boàty** |
| cup | **kàopy** |
| fork | **forsèty** |
| glass | **vèra** |
| plate | **lovìa, vilìa** |
| knife | **àntsy** |
| spoon | **sòtro** |
| teaspoon | **sòtro kèly** |
| toothpick | **fisokìra-nìfy** |

## ◆ Accommodations

For non-residents, lodging is generally required to be paid for in foreign currency. Simple establishments accept payment in Malagasy francs.

I am looking for ... .
  **Mitàdy ... àho.**
  a hotel
    **hôtèly**
  a bungalow
    **bungalow**
  a room
    **èfitra**
Where is ... ?
  **Àiza no mìsy ... ?**
  a campground
    **toèrana filasìna**
  a cheap hotel
    **hôtèly mòra**
  a good hotel
    **hôtèly tsàra**
  a clean hotel
    **hôtèly madìo**
  a nearby hotel
    **hôtèly akàiky**
  a hotel at/near the beach
    **hôtèly amòron-dranomàsina**
  a quiet hotel
    **hôtèly mangingìna**
Could you take me to the hotel ... ?
  **Àfaka mitòndra àhy àmin'ny hôtèly ... ve ianào?**
Can we camp here?
  **Àfaka milàsy èto ve?**

# ACCOMMODATIONS

Is it safe to camp here?
**Atokìsana ve ny milàsy èto?**

How long can we stay here?
**Hafirìana no àzo ijanònana èto?**

Can you watch over this place tonight?
**Àfaka miàmbina ity toèrana ity ve ianào anìo àlina?**

Is there drinking water?
**Mìsy ràno fisòtro ve èto?**

May we light a fire?
**Àfaka mampirèhitra àfo ve?**

Do you have any rooms free?
**Mbola mìsy èfitra ve?**

May we ... here?
**Àfaka ... èto ve?**

I have already booked a hotel/room.
**Èfa namàndrika hôtèly/èfitra àho.**

I would like ... .
**Mìla ... àho.**

a room
**èfitra**

a single room
**èfitra tòkana**

a double room
**èfitra ho an'olon-dròa**

for ... persons
**òlona ...**

for ... days/weeks
**... àndro /herinàndro**

with a balcony
**mìsy lavaràngana**

with a shower/bathroom
**mìsy fandròana**

with a TV
**mìsy telè**

with cold running water
**mìsy ràno**

with hot water
**mìsy ràno mafàna**

a room with air-conditioning
**èfitra climatisé**

with a telephone
**mìsy telefàonina**

with electricity
**mìsy jìro**

that is tidy
**madìo**

with a view of the sea
**mitòdika àmin'ny ranomàsina**

with a mosquito net
**mìsy voàly àro-mòka**

How much is it ... ?
**Ohatrìnona ... ?**

per day?
**ìsan'àndro?**

per person?
**ìsan'òlona?**

per week?
**ìsan-kerinàndro?**

May I speak to the manager?
**Afaka mirèsaka àmin'ny mpandraharàha àho ve?**

How long will you be staying?
**Hahàritra hafirìana ianarèo?**

one, two, three, four, five
**irày, ròa, tèlo, èfatra, dìmy**

... days.
**... àndro.**

a week
**herinàndro**

Do you have any I.D.?
>**Mànana kàra-panòndro ve ianào?**

My name is ... .
>**... no anàrako.**

Sorry, we are full.
>**Miàla tsìny fa èfa fèno izahày.**

All right.
>**Èny àry.**

Can I have the key to my room?
>**Àiza ny lakilè an'ny èfitro?**

Where is my room?
>**Àiza ny èfitro e?**

I need ... .
>**Mìla ... àho.**

Please wake me up at ... .
>**Mba tàiro àmin'ny ... àho.**

I would like to pay the bill.
>**Sàika handòa vòla àho.**

Do you accept credit cards?
>**Mandrày carte de crédit ve ianarèo?**

## WORDS

| | |
|---|---|
| accommodations | **tràno ivantànana** |
| backpack | **sac à dos** *fr* |
| bathroom | **fandròana** |
| bed | **fandrìana** |
| bill | **addition** *fr* |
| blanket | **bodofòtsy** |
| bottle | **tavoahàngy** |
| bucket | **sceau** *fr* |
| candle | **labozìa** |
| chair | **sèza** |
| clean *adj.* | **madìo** |
| clean sheets | **drà madìo** |

# ACCOMMODATIONS

| | |
|---|---|
| cold | mangatsìaka |
| cold water | ràno mangatsìaka |
| compass | famantàrana avàratra |
| cook *v.* | mahàndro |
| credit card | carte de crédit *fr* |
| dirty | malòto |
| to drink water | misòtro ràno |
| drinking water | ràno fisòtro |
| fire | àfo |
| hammer | maritò |
| hot | mafàna |
| hot water | ràno mafàna |
| included | èfa ào anàtiny |
| key | lakilè |
| lamp | jìro |
| light | jìro |
| mattress | kidòro |
| meals | sakàfo |
| mosquito net | voàly àro mòka |
| noisy | mitabatàba |
| pillow | òndana |
| plug | prìzy |
| quiet | mangìna |
| room | èfitra |
| room number | nimeràon'ny èfitra |
| rope | tàdy |
| sheet | làmba |
| shower | fandròana |
| sleep | matòry |
| soap | savòny |
| swim | milomàno |
| table | latàbatra |
| tent | tràno lày |
| toilet paper | papier hygiénique *fr* |
| towel | servièta |
| water | ràno |

Travel

*Transport*

**Public transportation** is crowded and poorly maintained. Buses do not pass by at regular times. In the capital Antananarivo, most people travel by privately-run mini-buses, **taxi be,** also named **jòno bòtry**. They are not very expensive (1000FMG to mid-2000) but are sometimes crowded. They also stop at bus stations.

You can get a taxi for yourself anywhere.

**The rail network** is very restricted. The main lines run between Antananarivo and Tamatave, Antananarivo and Antsirabe, Moramanga and Lac Alaotra, and Antananarivo and Ambatondrazaka. It is advisable to ask for the departure times. If the train is not fully booked, it will be canceled though you will not be informed. For this reason, very few local people travel by rail. **Taxi-brousses** (bush taxis) are popular, and connect the towns provided with rail service, mentioned above. **Taxi-brousses** are not very expensive and cover the distance in a shorter time. They can be picked up at special "car parks."

**Domestic flights** are only payable in foreign currency. They are always full and very often overbooked. There are no seat assignments. Make sure to reconfirm in advance every flight, otherwise your reservation will automatically be canceled. A small departure tax is charged on all flights.

## Inquiries

What time does the ... leave/arrive?
**Àmin'ny fìry no miàla/tònga ... ?**
Where can I take the ... to ... ?
**Àiza ny fakàna ... mankàny ... ?**

| | |
|---|---|
| the airplane | **ny raoplànina** |
| the boat | **ny sàmbo** |
| the bus | **ny bus** |
| the train | **ny masìnina** |
| the "taxi-brousse" | **ny taxi-brousse** |
| the "taxi be" | **ny taxi be, jòno bòtry** |

The ... is delayed.
**Tàra ny ... .**
The ... is canceled.
**Tsy mandèha ny ... .**
Where is the ticket office?
**Àiza ny fivaròtana biè?**
I want to go to ... .
**Sàika ho àny ... àho.**
I want a ticket to ... .
**Biè mankàny ... irày.**
A one-way ticket
**Biè mandròso**
A return ticket
**Biè mandròso sy mivèrina**
first class
**première classe** *fr*
second class
**deuxième classe** *fr*
Can I reserve a seat to ... ?
**Àfaka mamàndrika toèrana mankàny ... ve?**
How long does the trip take?
**Mahàritra hafirìana ny mankàny ... ?**

## By Plane

Is there a flight to ... today?
**Mìsy raoplànina mankàny ... ve anìo?**
When is the next flight to ... ?
**Rahovìana ny raoplànina manàraka
mankàny ... ?**
Is this the flight for ... ?
**Ity ve ny raoplànina mankàny ... ?**
Is that flight from ... ?
**Àvy àny ... ve ity raoplànina ity?**
When is the flight from ... arriving?
**Àmin'ny fìry ny raoplànina àvy àny ... no
tònga?**
Is it on time?
**Tònga àra-potòana ve?**
Do I have to change planes?
**Mìla miòva raoplànina ve àho?**
international flight
**vol international** *fr*
national flight
**vol intérieur** *fr*

## By Bus

Buses are not expensive (standard mid-2000: 500
FMG). They do not stop at all bus stops. If you want
to get off the bus at the next station, you have to
shout: **Mìsy miàla ào!** 'I want to get off there!', so
that the driver or the driver's assistant can hear you.
Sometimes the driver's assistant asks, **Mìsy miàla?**
'Does anyone wants to get off?' and you have to
answer **Mìsy miàla!**, if you want to get out.

ticket
**biè**

bus fare
**frais ana bus**
bus stop
**arè àna bus, fakàna bus (optionally)**
taxi brousse station
**arè ana taxi brousse, fakàna taxi brousse**
(optionally)
Where is the bus station?
**Àiza ny arè ana bus e?**
Which bus goes to ... ?
**Bus fìry no mankàny ... ?**
Does this bus go to ... ?
**Mankàny ... ve ity bus ity?**
Where do I have to get out if I want to go to ... ?
**Àiza àho no miàla ràha ho àny ... ?**
Will you let me know when we arrive at ... ?
**Làzainào àho ve rehèfa tònga ào ... ?**

## By Taxi

You can hail any taxi that is passing by. There is a standard taxi fare <u>within</u> the city for wherever you want to go (6000 FMG in mid-2000). Always ask the taxi driver for the fare before getting in.

fare
**frais** *fr*, **sàran-dàlana**
taxi fare
**frais àna taxi**
I am going to ... .
**Ho èny ... àho.**
How long will it take?
**Àdiny fìry ny mankàny?**
How much does it cost?
**Ohatrìnona ny mankàny?**

How much is the taxi fare now?
**Ohatrìnona ny frais taxi izào?**
Have you got change?
**Mànana madìnika ve ianào?**

## *Rikshaws*

Rikshaws are available for transport in two big
towns: Tamatave (on the eastern coast) and in
Antsirabe (in the central highlands). You can hail
any rikshaw driver passsing by. The rikshaw fare
within the city is standard and is not expensive but
you must expect to pay more than the local people.

## ◆ Trips and Sightseeing

Where do you want to go?
  **Àiza no tianào alèha?**
I would like to go to ... .
  **Sàika ho èny ... àho.**
I would like to see (the) ... .
  **Te-hahìta (ny) ... àho.**
Where is the ... ?
  **Àiza no mìsy ny ... ?**
Is this the ... ?
  **Ity ve ny ... ?**
How much is the entrance fee?
  **Ohatrìnona ny fidìrana?**
When can I visit the ... ?
  **Rahovìana no àzo jerèna ny ... ?**
I would like to go to the forest.
  **Te ho àny an'àla àho.**
I would like to visit a nature reserve.
  **Te ho àny àmin'ny réserves naturelles àho.**
I would like to go to the beach.
  **Te ho àny amòron-drànomàsina àho.**
I would like to go to the mountains.
  **Te ho àny an-tèndrombòhitra àho.**
Is it far from here?
  **Làvitra èto ve izàny?**
Can we go there on foot?
  **Tònga tòngotra ve àny?**
I would like to drive around the town.
  **Te-handèha hijèry tanàna àho.**
I would like to go for a walk.
  **Te-hitsangatsàngana àho.**
How do I get to ... ?
  **Ahòana no hahatongàvako àny ... ?**
  by "taxi-brousse"    **mandèha taxi brousse**
  by bicycle          **mandèha bisikilèta**

| | |
|---|---|
| by boat | **mandèha làkana** |
| by bus | **mandèha bus** |
| by cross-country car | **mandèha landrover** |
| by motorbike | **mandèha moto** |
| by plane | **mandèha ràoplànina** |
| by taxi | **mandèha taxi** |
| by train | **mandèha masìnina** |

How do I get to ... on foot?

**Ahòana no hahatongàvako tòngotra àny ... ?**

Which attractions are worth seeing in ... ?

**Ìnona no tsàra hohita àny ... ?**

Is it allowed to take photographs here?

**Àzo hakàna sàry ve èto?**

Is there a guide who can speak English?

**Mìsy gìda mahày mitèny anglìsy ve?**

Is that possible?

**Mèty hièty ve izàny?**

## WORDS

| | |
|---|---|
| attraction | **toèrana tsàra hìta** |
| beach | **amòron-drànomàsina** |
| bridge | **tetèzana** |
| building | **tràno** |
| capital | **rènivòhitra** |
| church | **fiangònana** |
| city center | **ville** *fr* |
| coast | **amòrontsìraka** |
| English language | **tèny anglìsy** |
| fair | **foàra** |
| festival | **festival** *fr* |
| garden | **zaridàina** |
| guide | **gìda** |
| harbor | **pôro, serànan-tsàmbo** |
| hospital | **hôpitàly** |

# TRIPS AND SIGHTSEEING

| | |
|---|---|
| hotel | **hôtèly** |
| house | **tràno** |
| island | **nòsy** |
| lake | **lac** |
| landscape | **paysage** *fr* |
| market | **tsèna** |
| mausoleum | **môsôlè** |
| monument | **tsàngam-bàto** |
| mountain | **tèndrombòhitra** |
| museum | **musée** *fr* |
| nature reserve | **réserves naturelles** *fr* |
| park | **zaridàina** |
| picnic | **fitsàngatsangànana** |
| railway station | **gàra** |
| river | **reniràno** |
| school | **fianàrana** |
| sea | **ranomàsina** |
| shop | **fivaròtana** |
| show | **exposition** *fr* |
| souvenir | **fahatsiaròvana** |
| stadium | **stade** *fr* |
| street | **làlana** |
| suburb | **manodìdina** |
| tomb | **fàsana** |
| university | **Oniversitè** |
| village | **ambànivòhitra** |
| visit | **fitsidìhina** |
| waterfall | **rìana** |
| zoo | **zoo** *fr* |

## Renting a Vehicle

I need a ... .
**Mìla ... àho.**

| | |
|---|---|
| car | **fiàra, fiàrakodìa, tômôbìlina** (optionally) |

| | |
|---|---|
| motorbike | **moto** *fr* |
| bike | **biskilèta** |
| cross-country vehicle | **landrover** *engl* |
| motorboat | **vedèty** |
| minibus | **minibus** *fr* |

Where can I rent a car?
> **Àiza no àfaka manòfa tômôbìlina?**

I would like to rent a car.
> **Sàika hanòfa tômôbìlina àho.**

I would like to go to ... .
> **Sàika handèha àny ... àho.**

Do you have a suitable car for these roads?
> **Mànana tômôbìlina mahavìta irèo làlana irèo ve ianào?**

I would like a car with a driver.
> **Sàika hanòfa tômôbìlina mìsy saofèra àho.**

I do not need a driver.
> **Tsy mìla saofèra àho.**

How much is that?
> **Ohatrìnona izàny?**

I need a car for ... persons.
> **Mìla tômôbìlina ho an'òlona ... àho.**

| | |
|---|---|
| for ... days | **... àndro** |
| for ... weeks | **... herinàndro** |
| for ... months | **... vòlana** |

Do you rent the car with a full tank of gas?
> **Mampanòfa tômôbìlina èfa fèno làsantsy ve ianarèo?**

When can I pick up the car?
> **Rahovìana no àzoko alàina ilày tomôbìlina?**

Do I have to pay the insurance?
> **Mìla mandòa assurance ve àho?**

You must pay a deposit.
> **Mìla mandòa avànsa ianào.**

# TRIPS AND SIGHTSEEING

What should I do if the car breaks down?
   **Ìnona no atàoko ràha sìmba ny tomôbìlina?**
Would you pay for the car repair?
   **Alòanareo ve ny làny?**
Your driver's license, please!
   **Ny permis anào azafàdy e.**
Your passport, please!
   **Ny pasipàorinào azafàdy!**

## WORDS

| | |
|---|---|
| car | **fiàra, fiarakodìa, tômôbìlina** |
| cross-country car | **landrover, tout-terrain** *fr* |
| deposit | **avànsa** |
| driver | **mpamìly, saofèra** |
| driver's license | **permis** *fr* |
| for a day | **àndro irày** |
| for a week | **herinàndro** |
| for a month | **irày vòlana** |
| gas | **làsantsy** |
| gas container | **fasìana lasàntsy** |
| hired car | **voiture de location** *fr*, **tômôbìlina nofàina** |
| insurance | **assurance** *fr* |
| motorbike | **moto** *fr* |
| oil | **mènaka** |
| per day | **ìsan'àndro** |
| per week | **ìsan-kerinàndro** |
| per month | **ìsam-bòlana** |
| street | **arabè, làlana** |
| to pay | **mandòa vòla** |
| to pay a deposit | **mandòa avànsa** |
| traffic | **circulation** *fr* |
| trip | **dìa** |

◆ **Directions**

Excuse me!
    **Azafàdy e!**
I would like to go to ... .
    **Sàika ho àny ... àho.**
Where is the ... ?
    **Àiza no mìsy ny ... ?**
Do you know where the ... is?
    **Fantatrào ve àiza ny ... ?**
Do you know where ... is?
    **Fantatrào ve àiza ho àiza no mìsy**
        **an' i ... (name of a place)?**
How long does it take to go to ... ?
    **Àdiny firy ny làlana mankàny ... ?**
Is this the right way to ... ?
    **Ity ve ny làlana mankàny ... ?**
Which bus goes to ... ?
    **Bus firy no mankàny ... ?**
You can take the bus number ... .
    **Bus ... ràisina.**
Where do I get off the bus?
    **Àiza àho no miàla bus?**
You can go there on foot.
    **Azonào handehànana tòngotra mankàny.**
Turn right at the corner.
    **Miodìna ankavànana ètsy àmin'ny sìsin-**
        **dàlana ètsy.**
Turn left at the corner.
    **Miodìna ankavìa ètsy àmin'ny sìsin-dàlana**
        **ètsy.**
Just go straight.
    **Mandehàna mahìtsy àny fòana.**
Go back.
    **Miverèna.**

Turn around.
**Miodìna.**
You are on the wrong way.
**Dìso làlana ianào.**
I am lost.
**Vèry àho.**
It is not far.
**Tsy làvitra ìo.**
It is very far from here.
**Làvitra be èto ìo.**

## Words

| | |
|---|---|
| across | **èo am-pìta** |
| behind | **èo am-bàdika** |
| besides | **akàiky** |
| bus station | **arè bus** |
| east | **atsinànana** |
| in front of | **manolòana ny** |
| left | **ankavìa** |
| north | **avàratra** |
| on foot | **mandèha an-tòngotra** |
| past the ... | **àorian'ny ...** |
| right | **ankavànana** |
| south | **atsìmo** |
| straight | **mahìtsy be** |
| west | **andrèfana** |

# COMMUNICATIONS

## ◆ Communications

You can make a phone call to foreign countries from any public phone as well as from the post office. You need a phone card for the call.

I would like to make a phone call.
**Sàika hiàntso telefàonina àho.**
I would like a telephone card.
**Mìla télécarte àho.**
What is the area code for ... ?
**Ìnona ny indicatif an'i ... ?**
I would like to send a fax to ... .
**Sàika handèfa fax àny ... àho.**
How much does a phone call to ... cost?
**Ohatrìnona ny miàntso telefàonina àny ... ?**
How much does a telephone card cost?
**Ohatrìnona ny télécarte iràry?**
Where is the nearest public phone?
**Àiza ny publiphone akàiky indrìndra èto?**
Where is a nearby post office?
**Àiza ny pàositra akàiky èto?**
What time does the post office open?
**Àmin'ny fìry no misòkatra ny pàositra?**
What time does the post office close?
**Àmin'ny fìry no mikàtona ny pàositra?**
Where is the mail box?
**Àiza ny fandrotsàhana taratàsy?**
How much does it cost to send this to ... ?
**Ohatrìnona ny mandèfa an'ity àny ... ?**

| | |
|---|---|
| Austria | **Ôtrìsy** |
| England | **Angletèra** |
| France | **Fràntsa** |
| Germany | **Alemàina** |
| the United States | **Amerìka** |

(The names of the English-speaking African countries are the same as in English.)

I would like some stamps.
> **Mìla tàmbra àho.**

I would like to send a ... .
> **Sàika handèfa ... àho.**

| | |
|---|---|
| letter | **taratàsy** |
| postcard | **kàrta** |
| parcel | **pakè** |
| telegram | **telegràma** |

How quicky can this arrive?
> **Hafirìana no tònga ity?**

*'Priority mail' does not exist in Madagascar.*

Where can I get Internet-connection?
> **Àiza no mèty ahazòako mampiàsa Internet?**
> > (Public internet access exists in large cities.)

Where can I send out e-mail?
> **Àiza no àzoko andefàsana e-mail?**

## WORDS

| | |
|---|---|
| airmail | **par avion** *fr* |
| communication | **fifandràisana** |
| e-mail | **lettre éléctronique** *fr* |
| | or **e-mail** |
| envelope | **valòpy** |
| fax | **fax** *fr* |
| mail box | **fandrotsàhana taratàsy** |
| parcel/package | **pakè** |
| phone call | **telefàonina** |
| phone card | **télécarte** *fr* |
| post office | **pàositra** |
| public phone | **publiphone** *fr* |
| registered mail | **rekômandè** |
| stamp | **tàmbra, hajìa** |
| telegram | **telegràma** |

# COMMUNICATIONS

| | |
|---|---|
| telephone | **telefàonina** |
| telephone card | **télécarte** *fr* |
| telephone connection | **fifandràisana an-tariby** |
| to send | **mandèfa** |

## ◆ Shopping

A wide and wonderful variety of handmade objects in wood, horn, metal, leather, stone, clay, stone, etc. can be bought on Malagasy markets. Keep in mind that there are many items which require authorizations. Ask the sellers each time you buy Malagasy handicrafts if you need an authorization for the items you have bought. The sellers can give you a "certificat de vente," a form describing the products sold and its price. Before leaving Madagascar, you may be asked by the customs officer at the airport to show the form. It is prohibited to transport internationally many items such as crocodile leather and endemic plants. Check with your travel agency or the Malagasy embassy in your country about these regulations before traveling.

It is a typical Malagasy behavior to negotiate prices at markets (though not in supermarkets). The sellers always set the prices at much higher than the actual value of the items since bargaining is always expected. It is advisable to offer a lower price than the first given price and then increase it in small amounts.

French numbers (un, deux, trois, quatre, etc.) are more often used in pricing than Malagasy numbers. Make sure the item you buy is in good condition. Bought items are generally nonrefundable and nonreturnable.

Credit cards are slowly gaining acceptance but their usage is still very limited. Credit cards are not accepted in markets or supermarkets. Only a few major hotels and a few travel agencies accept them.

# SHOPPING

Where can I find a ... ?
   **Àiza no mèty mìsy ... ?**
Where is the market?
   **Àiza no mìsy ny tsèna?**
Where is the nearest ... ?
   **Àiza ny ... akàiky indrìndra?**
· What can I do for you?
   **Ìnona no atào ho anào?**
Could you show me some ... ?
   **Àfaka mampisèho ... àhy ve ianào?**
Do you have ... ?
   **Mìsy ... ve?**
Do you have any others?
   **Mbòla mìsy hàfa ve?**
I do not like this.
   **Tsy tìako ity.**
Do you have anything bigger/smaller?
   **Mìsy lehibebè/kelikèly nòho ity ve?**
Do you have a different color?
   **Mìsy lòko hàfa ve?**
Do you have more?
   **Mbòla mìsy hàfa ve?**
I would like to buy this.
   **Tìako vidìana ity.**
How much is this/that?
   **Ohatrìnona ity/iry e?**
That is too expensive.
   **Làfo be izàny.**
How about ... (lower price)?
   **Mèty ... ve?**
What is your last price?
   **Ohatrìnona ny fàrany?**
That is my very last price.
   **Izày mihìtsy ny fàrany.**
That is still expensive for me.
   **Mbòla làfo àmiko izàny.**

I will take it for ... francs.
   **Hoèntiko ràha ... Francs.**
Thank you, good-bye.
   **Misàotra àry fa velòma.**


## Places

| | |
|---|---|
| bakery | **mpivàrotra mòfo** |
| bookstore | **fivaròtam-bòky** |
| butcher | **fivaròtan-kèna** |
| clothing store | **fivaròtan'akànjo** |
| florist | **mpivàro-boninkàzo** |
| greengrocer | **mpivàrotr'ànana** |
| jeweler | **mpanào firàvaka,** |
| | **bijoutier** *fr* |
| kiosk | **kiosque** *fr* |
| market | **tsèna** |
| pharmacy | **pharmacie** *fr,* **farmasìa** |
| shop | **fivaròtana** |
| souvenir shop | **mpivàrotra sovenìra** |
| supermarket | **supermarché** *fr* |
| tailor | **mpanjàitra, couturier** *fr* |
| travel agent | **agence de bureau** *fr* |
| watchmaker | **mpanào famantaranàndro** |


## Words

| | |
|---|---|
| bag, basket | **hàrona** |
| bathing suit | **maillot de bain** *fr* |
| belt | **fehikìbo** |
| book(s) | **bòky** |
| box | **boàty** |
| bracelet | **braselè** |
| cardigan | **akànjo bà** |

| | |
|---|---|
| dress | **akànjo** |
| earrings | **kàvina** |
| flower(s) | **voninkàzo** |
| gloves | **gants** *fr* |
| gold | **volamèna** |
| handbag | **paokètra** |
| handcraft | **àsa tànana** |
| handkerchief | **mosàra** |
| hat | **sàtroka** |
| leather | **hòditra** |
| metal | **vy** |
| necklace | **ròjo** |
| pants | **patalòha** |
| pottery | **tèfy tanimànga** |
| raincoat | **imper** *fr* |
| ring | **pèratra** |
| sandals | **kàpa** |
| scarf | **folàra** |
| shirt | **lòbaka** |
| shoes | **kiràro** |
| silver | **volafòtsy** |
| souvenirs | **fahatsiaròvana** |
| stockings, socks | **bà** |
| stone | **vàto** |
| tablecloth | **làmba-datàbatra** |
| T-shirt | **T-shirt** |
| umbrella | **èlo** |
| vase | **vàzy** |
| watch | **famantaranàndro** |

## ◆ Money

The Malagasy currency is Franc Malgache, abbreviated as FMG or the popularly-used unit **ariàry**. One **ariàry** equals five francs. In mid-year 2000, $1.00 bought 6400 FMG.

FMG are bought at banks, exchange counters in hotels and at the Ivato airport. The banks' exchange rate is more favorable than the hotels'.

Foreign currency must be declared on arrival.

Where is the nearest bank?
   **Aiza ny bànky akàiky indrìndra èto?**
Where can I change some money?
   **Àiza no àfaka manakàlo vòla?**
When is the bank open?
   **Àmin'ny fìry ny bànky no misòkatra?**
When does the bank close?
   **Àmin'ny fìry ny bànky no mihìdy?**
I want to change some dollars/pounds.
   **Sàika hanakàlo dôlàra/livre sterling àho.**
Can you give me some small change?
   **Àfaka manomè vòla madìnika ve ianào?**
I want to cash this check.
   **Sàika hanakàlo chèque àho.**
How much are ... dollars in Malagasy Francs?
   **Ohatrìnona ny ... dôlàra àmin'ny vòla gàsy?**
What is the exchange rate today?
   **Ohatrìnona ny cours anìo?**
Your passport, please.
   **Ny pasipàronào azafàdy.**
Please sign here.
   **Soniàvo kèly èto azafàdy.**

## WORDS

| | |
|---|---|
| amount | **montant** *fr* (the total) |
| bank | **bànky** |
| banknote | **vòla taratàsy** |
| cash | **espèces** *fr*, **tòlo-bòtsotra** |
| cashier | **caisse** *fr*, **guichet** *fr* |
| check | **chèque** *fr* |
| coins | **vòla madìnika** |
| exchange rate | **cours** *fr*, **sàndam-bòla** |
| dollar | **dôlàra** |
| foreign currency | **devises** *fr*, **vòla vahìny** |
| form | **taratàsy fenòina,** **formulaire** *fr* |
| pound | **livre sterling** *fr* |
| money | **vòla** |
| payment | **paiement** *fr*, **fandoàvam-bòla** |
| signature | **sonìa** |
| small change | **vòla madìnika** |
| to buy | **mivìdy** |
| to change | **manakàlo vòla** |
| to pay | **mandòa vòla** |
| to sign | **manào sonìa** |
| to trade | **manào vàrotra** |
| to withdraw money | **màka vòla** |
| traveler's check | **chèque de voyage** *fr* |

## ◆ Health

Madagascar is a subtropical country where **malaria** is a serious problem. It is best to consult your doctor before your trip. Malaria medicines generally have to be taken a few days before your departure and have to be continued after your return. Vaccinations against hepatitis A and tetanus are advisable. A yellow fever vaccination certificate is required for travelers from African countries.

It is recommended to bring your own one-way syringes and needles.

Water used for drinking, brushing one's teeth or making ice should have first been boiled or sterilized. Meat, fish and vegetables should be well cooked. Dairy products that are likely to have been made from unboiled milk should be avoided.

Public and private medical care services are available. It is recommended to seek private doctors and hospitals though they often request immediate cash payment for health care services. All medications are not always available. You should bring any specific medicine that you require.

### At the Doctor's

I am sick.
   **Maràry àho.**
My friend is sick.
   **Maràry ny nàmako.**
I do not feel well.
   **Tsy metimèty àho.**

I feel nauseous.
**Maloilòy àho.**

This person is sick.
**Maràry ity òlona ity.**

I need a doctor.
**Mìla dokotera àho.**

My ... hurt(s).
**Maràry ny ... -ko.**

It hurts here.
**Èto no maràry.**

I have a problem with my ... .
**Mìsy tsy mèty ny ... -ko.**

I am allergic to ... .
**Tsy mahazàka ... àho.**

I have vomited.
**Nandòa àho.**

I feel dizzy.
**Fànina àho.**

I cannot sleep.
**Tsy mahìta tòry àho.**

I cannot eat.
**Tsy mahìnan-kànina àho.**

I am pregnant.
**Bevohòka àho.**

I have a cold.
**Vòan'ny grìpa àho.**

I have a temperature.
**Mamày àho.**

I have a cough.
**Mikòhaka àho.**

I have a headache.
**Maràry an-dòha àho.**

I have a broken leg.
**Tàpaka ny tòngotro.**

I have a broken arm.
**Tàpaka ny tànako.**

I have diarrhea.
**Mivàlana àho.**

I am constipated.
**Mitòhana àho.**

I have a backache.
**Maràry lamòsina àho.**

Which pharmacy is open tonight?
**Farmasia ìza no misòkatra anìo àlina?**

I need medication for ... .
**Mìla fanafòdy ... àho.**

I have my own syringe.
**Mànana fanindrònana àho.**

How long/How often do I take this medication?
**Hafirìana/Im-pìry no hihinànako ity fanafòdy ity?**

You have a fever.
**Mìsy tàzo ianào.**

You have an infection.
**Mìsy infection ianào.**

It is contagious.
**Mamìndra ìo.**

Take this medication.
**Mihinàna ity fanafòdy ity ianào.**

## Specialists

| | |
|---|---|
| cardiologist | **spesialìsta fo** |
| dentist | **dokotèra nìfy, dentiste** *fr* |
| dermatologist | **dokotèra hòditra** |
| doctor | **dokotèra** |
| gynecologist | **dokotèram-behivàvy** |
| optometrist | **dokotèra màso** |
| pediatrician | **dokotèran-jàzakèly** |
| specialist | **spesialìsta** |
| surgeon | **mpandìdy** |

# HEALTH

## Diseases

| | |
|---|---|
| AIDS | **SIDA** |
| bacteria | **bakterìa** |
| cramps | **kràmpy** |
| diarrhea | **fivalànana** |
| epidemic | **arèti-mifìndra** |
| fever | **tàzo** |
| flu | **grìpa** |
| frostbite | **be mangòvitra** |
| headache | **arètin'andòha** |
| heart attack | **crise cardiaque** *fr* |
| hepatitis | **hepatìta** |
| high blood pressure | **ambòny tòsi-drà** |
| infection | **infection** *fr* |
| infectious | **mifìndra** |
| low blood pressure | **ambàny tòsi-drà** |
| malaria | **malarià** |
| parasite | **parazìta** |
| snakebite | **kàikitra bibilàva** |
| sore throat | **arètin-tènda** |
| stomachache | **arètim-bavòny** |
| toothache | **arèti-nìfy** |

## Parts of the Body

| | |
|---|---|
| ankle | **kìtrokèly** |
| arm | **sàndry** |
| back | **lamòsina** |
| blood | **ra** |
| body | **vàtana** |
| bone | **tàolana** |
| brain | **ati-dòha** |
| breast | **nòno** |
| cheek | **takòlaka** |

| | |
|---|---|
| chest | **tràtra** |
| chin | **sàoka** |
| ear | **sòfina** |
| elbow | **kìho** |
| eye | **màso** |
| face | **tarèhy** |
| finger | **ràntsana** |
| foot | **tòngotra** |
| forehead | **àndrina** |
| gums | **akànjo-nìfy** |
| hair | **vòlo** |
| hand | **tànana** |
| head | **lòha** |
| heart | **fo** |
| heel | **faladìa** |
| hip | **valàhana** |
| intestine | **tsinày** |
| jaw | **hìhy** |
| knee | **lohàlika** |
| leg | **tòngotra** |
| lip | **mòlotra** |
| liver | **àty** |
| lung | **avokàvoka** |
| mouth | **vàva** |
| nail | **hòho** |
| neck | **àtoka** |
| nose | **òrona** |
| palm | **tànana** |
| ribs | **tàolan-tehèzana** |
| shoulders | **sòroka** |
| skin | **hòditra** |
| stomach | **vavòny** |
| thigh | **fe** |
| throat | **tènda** |
| thumb | **ankihibè** |
| toe | **ràntsan-tòngotra** |

| | |
|---|---|
| tongue | **lèla** |
| tooth | **nìfy** |
| uterus | **trànon-jàza** |
| vein | **làlan-dra** |
| wrist | **valàhana** |

## Medication

| | |
|---|---|
| anesthetic | **anestezìa** |
| antibiotics | **antibiôtìka** |
| antidote, antitoxin | **òdy pòizina** |
| aspirin | **aspirìnina** |
| Band-Aid | **sparadrap** *fr* |
| cotton wool | **vovò** |
| cream | **paomàdy** |
| drops | **gòty** |
| injection | **tsìndrona** |
| medicines | **fanafòdy** |
| pharmacy | **farmasìa, pharmacie** *fr* |
| on call pharmacy | **farmasìa gàrda** |
| pills | **pìla** |
| powder | **vòvoka** |
| quinine | **kinìnina** |
| soporific | **fanafòdy fampatorìana** |
| suppository | **suppo** *fr*, **fanafòdy asìsika** |
| syringe | **tsìndrona** |
| thermometer | **termômètatra** |
| tranquilizer | **calmant** *fr* |
| vitamin | **vitamìnina** |

## ◆ Administration

### *Filling Out Forms*

Can you fill out this form please?
>  **Fenòy kèly ity azafàdy.** (Fill this out please.)

What is your name?
>  **Ìza no anaranào?**

My name is … .
>  **… no anàrako.**

When were you born?
>  **Ovìana ianào no tèraka?**

I was born in … .
>  **Tèraka tàmin'ny … àho.**

Where do you come from?
>  **Àvy àiza ianào?**

I come from … .
>  **Àvy àny … àho.**

| | |
|---|---|
| America | **Amerìka** |
| Australia | **Aostralìa** |
| Austria | **Otrìsy** |
| England | **Angletèra** |
| Switzerland | **Soìsy** |

Where do you want to go?
>  **Àiza no tianào halèha?**

What is your address in Madagascar?
>  **Àiza ny adiresinào èto Madagasikàra?**

Are you here for business or for vacation?
>  **Hiàsa èto ianào sa hàka rìvotra?**

How long are you staying in Madagascar?
>  **Hafirìana no hijanònanào èto Madagasikàra?**

I am staying in Madagascar for … days/weeks/
months.
>  **Mijànona … àndro/herinàndro/vòlana èto
>  Madagasikàra àho.**

# ADMINISTRATION

Do I need an authorization for ... ?
**Mìla autorisation ve àho ràha mankàny ... ?**
What does this mean?
**Ìnona no dìkan'ity?**
What does ... mean?
**Ìnona no dìkan'ny hoè ... ?**
Where is ...'s office?
**Àiza ny biràon'i ... ?**
I would like to apply for an authorization to ... .
**Sàika hangàtaka autorisation àmin'ny ... àho.**

| | |
|---|---|
| for one person | **ho an'òlona irày** |
| for two persons | **ho an'òlon-dròa** |
| for all of us | **ho anày rehètra** |

How much does an authorization cost?
**Ohatrìnona ny autorisation irày?**
An authorization costs ... FMG.
**... FMG./... FMG ny autorisation.**
Is there anything we should particularly pay attention to?
**Mìsy zàvatra tòkony hotandrèmanay manòkana ve?**
Please sign here.
**Soniàvo èto azafàdy.**

Most of the forms you encounter will be written either in French or in Malagasy. Sometimes they are written in both languages.

## WORDS

| | |
|---|---|
| application form | **taratàsy fangatàhana** |
| surname | **anàrana** |
| first name | **fanàmpin'anàrana** |
| date of birth | **dàty nahateràhana** |

| | |
|---|---|
| place of birth | **toèrana nahateràhana** |
| male/female | **lahy/vavy** |
| married/single | **manambàdy/tsy manambàdy** |
| profession | **àsa** |
| address | **adirèsy** |
| nationality | **fihavìana** |
| reason for travel | **ànton-dìa** |
| business | **raharàha** |
| tourism | **fizahàn-tàny** |
| work | **àsa** |
| single | **tsy mbòla manambàdy** |
| married | **manam-bàdy** |
| divorced | **nisàra-panambadìana** |
| date of arrival | **dàty nahatongàvana** |
| date of departure | **dàty hiverènana** |
| passport | **pasipàoro** |
| passport number | **nimeràon'ny pasipàoro** |
| passport photograph | **sàry tàpaka** |
| a copy of | **kôpìan'ny** |
| signature | **sonìa** |
| valid | **mànan-kèry** |
| visa | **visa** *fr* |

## Ministry

| | |
|---|---|
| Ministry of ... | **minìstry ny ...** |
| Agriculture | **fambolèna** |
| Defense | **fiaròvana** |
| Education | **fampianàrana** |
| Foreign Affairs | **raharàham-bahìny** |
| Health | **fahasalamàna** |
| Home Affairs | **ati-tàny** |
| Justice | **fitsaràna** |
| Transport | **fitatèrana** |
| Water and Forests | **ràno sy àla** |

# WEATHER

## ◆ Weather

The best season to visit Madagascar is from May to October. In fact, most of the rain falls from November to April.

Temperature is measured in degrees celcius.
$^\circ C = 5/9 (F^\circ -32)$

How is the weather?
**Manahòana ny àndro?**
What will the weather be like tomorrow?
**Hanào ahòana ny àndro rahampìtso?**
The weather is bad.
**Ràtsy ny àndro.**
The weather is beautiful.
**Tsàra ny àndro.**
The sun shines.
**Mipòaka ny masoàndro.**
It is lightning.
**Mitsèlatra.**
It is thundering.
**Mikòtroka.**
It is hailing.
**Mìsy avàndra.**
It is very cold.
**Mangatsìaka be ny àndro.**
It is very warm.
**Mafàna be ny àndro.**
It is ... degrees.
**... degrè. (Celcius)**
It is cloudy.
**Mandràhona ny àndro.**
It is foggy.
**Manjàvona ny àndro.**

It is raining.
**Àvy ny òrana.**
It is going to rain.
**Ho àvy ny òrana.**
Take an umbrella!
**Mitondrà èlo!**
Put on warm clothing!
**Manàova akànjo mafàna!**

## Words

| | |
|---|---|
| cloudy | **mandràhona** |
| cold | **mangatsìaka** |
| degree centigrade | **degrè** |
| flood | **tòndra-dràno** |
| fog | **zàvona** |
| hail *n.* | **avàndra** |
| lightning | **tsèlatra** |
| rain *n.* | **òrana** |
| thunder | **kòtroka** |
| thundershower | **òram-bàratra** |
| warm | **mamày** |

Nature

What is this?
**Ìnona ity?**
I would like to see a/an … .
**Te-hahìta … àho.**
It is a … .
**… ìo.**
Is it poisonous?
**Mìsy pòizina ve ìo?**
Is it dangerous to touch it?
**Mampìdi-dòza ve ny mikàsika an'io?**
Do you see that?
**Hìtanào ve ìo?**
Do you hear that?
**Hènonào ve izàny?**
I would like to climb it/hike it.
**Te-hanànika an'ìo àho.**
I would like to swim/walk.
**Te-hilomàno / handehandèha àho.**

## WORDS

| | |
|---|---|
| air | **rìvotra** |
| animal | **bìby** |
| brook | **reniràno kèly** |
| cloud | **ràhona** |
| cyclone | **rìvo-dòza** |
| desert | **èfitra** |
| dew | **àndo** |
| dust | **vòvoka** |
| dusty | **mamòvoka** |
| earthquake | **horohòron-tàny** |
| field | **tànim-bòly** |
| fire | **àfo** |

| | |
|---|---|
| flood | **tòndra-dràno** |
| flower | **voninkàzo** |
| forest | **àla** |
| fresh air | **rìvotra madìo** |
| full moon | **diavòlana** |
| hail | **avàndra** |
| heat | **hafanàna** |
| hill | **havòana** |
| landscape | **paysage** *fr* |
| lightning | **tsèlatra** |
| meadow | **fàhitra** |
| moon | **vòlana** |
| mud | **fòtaka** |
| nature | **zàva-manan'àina** |
| ocean | **oseànina** |
| palm tree | **palmiè** |
| plants | **zàva-manìry** |
| poison | **pòizina** |
| rain | **òrana** |
| rainbow | **àntsiben'Andriamànitra** |
| river | **reniràno** |
| sand | **fàsika** |
| sky | **lànitra** |
| smoke | **sètroka** |
| star | **kìntana** |
| storm | **tafìo-drìvotra** |
| sun | **masoàndro** |
| sunrise | **fiposàhan'ny masoàndro** |
| sunset | **fodìan'ny masoàndro** |
| sunshine | **tàna-masoàndro** |
| thunder | **kòtro-bàratra** |
| tree | **hàzo** |
| valley | **lohasàha** |
| view | **izày tàzana** |
| water | **ràno** |

# NATURE

| | |
|---|---|
| waterfall | **rìana** |
| wind | **rìvotra** |

## Animals

| | |
|---|---|
| ant | **vìtsika** |
| bee | **tantèly** |
| bird | **vòrona** |
| bull | **ombilàhy** |
| butterfly | **lòlo** |
| cat | **sàka** |
| caterpillar | **fandày** |
| chick | **akòhokèly** |
| chicken | **akòho** |
| cockroach | **kadràdraka** |
| cow | **òmby** |
| crocodile | **voày** |
| crow | **akoholàhy** |
| dog | **alìka** |
| donkey | **ampòndra** |
| duck | **gàna, ganagàna** |
| eagle | **vòromahèry** |
| eel | **amàlona** |
| elephant | **elefàntra** |
| fish | **tròndro** |
| flea | **paràsy** |
| fly | **làlitra** |
| frog | **sàhona** |
| gecko | **tanafisaka** |
| goat | **òsy** |
| goose | **gìsa** |
| herd | **andìam-bìby** |
| horse | **soavàly** |
| insect | **bìbikèly** |
| lamb | **zànak'òndry** |

| | |
|---|---|
| lemur | **gìdro*** |
| lion | **lìona** |
| monkey | **gìdro** |
| mosquito | **mòka** |
| mouse | **voalàvo** |
| owl | **vorondòlo** |
| pig | **kisòa** |
| rabbit | **bìtro** |
| rat | **voalàvo** |
| sheep | **òndry** |
| snail | **sìfotra** |
| snake | **bibilàva** |
| spider | **àla** |
| tiger | **tìgra** |
| turkey | **vorontsilòza** |
| turtle | **sòkatra** |
| wasp | **fanènitra** |
| wolf | **amboadìa** |
| worm | **kànkana** |

*\*Lemurs* are only found in Madagascar and on the Comoro Islands. Due to deforestation, some species are in danger of extinction. Lemurs range in size from the mouse lemurs (about 60 g) to the size of a large cat. The most familiar lemurs are the brown lemur, golden bamboo lemur (on the cover), grey bamboo lemur, grey mouse lemur, Sifaka, Indri indri and Aye-aye.

## Plants

| | |
|---|---|
| aloe | **vàhona** |
| bamboo | **bambò** |
| baobab | **baobàba** |
| bougainvillea | **làingomèna** |

| | |
|---|---|
| branch | **rantsan-kàzo** |
| burr | **tsipòlitra** |
| cinnamon | **kanèlina** |
| clove | **jiròfo** |
| coconut | **kôkô** |
| cotton | **landihàzo** |
| flower | **voninkàzo** |
| ginger | **sakamalàho** |
| grass | **bòzaka** |
| maize | **kàtsaka** |
| mushroom | **òlatra** |
| orchid | **orkidè** |
| pepper | **dipoàvatra** |
| plant | **zàva-manìry** |
| rose | **ràozy** |
| stem | **tàho** |
| sugarcane | **fàry** |
| thorn | **tsìlo** |
| tree | **hàzo** |
| vanilla | **vanìla** |
| water lily | **voahìrana** |

*Ravinala* is one of the plant emblems of Madagascar. It is a tree found in the forest, that looks like a banana tree. It is called 'the traveler's tree' because its trunk contains a supply of pure water that travelers and wanderers would drink.

## ◆ Politics

The state is a republic, named the "Republic of Madagascar" and based on a democracy.

The Republic of Madagascar's motto is: "Homeland — Revolution—Liberty."

### Words

| | |
|---|---|
| aid | **fanampìana** |
| ambassador | **ambasadèra** |
| arrest *v.* | **misàmbotra** |
| assembly | **fihàonana, fivorìana** |
| autonomy | **fahaleòvan-tèna** |
| charity | **fiantràna** |
| citizen | **òlon-tsòtra** |
| civil rights | **zo** |
| constitution | **lalàm-panorènana** |
| corruption | **fandràisana tsòlotra** |
| coup d'état | **coup d'état** *fr,* **fanongànam-panjakàna** |
| court of law | **fitsaràna** |
| crime | **hèloka, fandikàna lalàna** |
| criminal | **mèloka, mpandìka lalàna** |
| crisis | **krìzy** |
| debt | **tròsa** |
| democracy | **demôkrasìa** |
| diplomatic ties | **fifandràisana àra-diplômatìka** |
| election | **fifidiànana** |
| embassy | **ambasàdy** |
| free *adj.* | **àfaka** |
| freedom | **fahafàhana** |
| government | **governemànta** |

| | |
|---|---|
| human rights | zòn'olombèlona |
| independence | fahaleòvan-tèna |
| independent | mahalèo tèna |
| judge | mpitsàra |
| killer | mpamòno òlona |
| law | lalàna |
| lawyer | mpanào lalàna |
| leader | mpitàrika |
| liberation | famotsòrana |
| majority | ny màro an'ìsa |
| meeting | fivorìana |
| minister | minìstra |
| ministry | ministèra |
| minority | ny vìtsy an'ìsa |
| murder *n.* | mpamòno òlona |
| newspaper | gazèty |
| opposition | mpanòhitra |
| parliament | parlemànta |
| peace | fandrìam-pahalèmana |
| political party | antòko pôlitìka |
| politician | mpanào pôlitìka |
| politics | pôlitìka |
| president | prezidà |
| prime minister | premier ministre *fr* |
| prison | figadràna |
| protest *n.* | fanohèrana |
| radio | radiô |
| revolution | revôlisiôna |
| robbery | fandrobàna |
| spy *n.* | mpitsikìlo |
| struggle *v.* | mièzaka màfy; *n.* èzaka màfy |
| theft | hàlatra |
| veto *n.* | làtsabàto |
| vote *n.* | mandàtsa-bàto |

## ◆ Emergencies

### *Accidents*

There has been an accident.
**Mìsy aksidà àtsy.**

Does anyone speak English?
**Mìsy mitèny anglìsy ve?**

Can you help me?
**Àfaka manàmpy àhy ve ianào?**

Can you deal with the injured passengers?
**Àfaka mikarakàra irèo maràtra ve ianào?**

Can you call the police?
**Àfaka miàntso pôlìsy ve ianào?**

Can you call a doctor?
**Àfaka miàntso dokotèra ve ianào?**

Take me to the nearest hospital.
**Ènto àmin'ny hôpitàly akàiky indrìndra àho.**

Take me to a doctor.
**Ènto dokotèra àho.**

Is there a doctor among you?
**Mìsy dokotèra ve aminarèo?**

I am hurt.
**Maràtra àho.**

I am ill.
**Maràry àho.**

Can you give me your name and address?
**Omèo kèly ny anàrana sy ny adirèsinào àho.**

Can you show me your I.D.?
**Asehòy àhy kèly ny kara-panòndronào?**

### *Car Breakdown*

The ... is damaged.
**Sìmba ny ... .**

Where is the nearest garage?
**Àiza ny garage akàiky indrìndra?**
Can you tow me?
**Àfaka mitàrika àhy ve ianào?**
I have run out of gas.
**Làny lasàntsy àho.**
The car has a flat tire.
**Vàky ponè ny fiàra/fiàrakodìa/tômôbìlina.**
Where is the nearest gas station?
**Àiza ny mpivàrotra lasàntsy akàiky èto?**
Our car is stuck.
**Mihìtsoka ny fiàranày.**
We need a mechanic.
**Mìla mécanicien izahày.**
Check the oil/gas/battery.
**Mba jerèo aniè ny mènaka/ny lasàntsy/ny baterìa.**
There is something wrong with that car.
**Mìsy tsy miàdy ìo fiàra ìo.**

WORDS

| | |
|---|---|
| accelerator | **accelérateur** *fr* |
| air | **rìvotra** |
| battery | **baterìa** |
| brake | **freins** *fr* |
| breakdown | **fahasimbàna** |
| car | **fiàra, fiàrakodìa, tômôbìlina** (optionally) |
| clutch | **embrayage** *fr* |
| doctor | **dokotèra** |
| driver | **mpamìly, saofèra** |
| engine | **maotèra** |
| gasoline | **lasàntsy** |
| gear | **vitèsy** |

| hospital | **hôpitàly** |
| hurt | **maràtra** |
| mechanic | **mécanicien** *fr* |
| oil | **mènaka** |
| passenger | **mpandèha** |
| petrol | **lasàntsy** |
| radiator | **radiateur** *fr* |
| seat | **sèza** |
| spare tire | **roue de secours** *fr* |
| speed | **hafaingànam-pàndeha** |
| starter | **démarreur** *fr* |
| steering wheel | **volant** *fr* |
| tank | **fitoèran-dasàntsy** |
| tow | **mitàrika** |
| towrope | **tàdy fitarìtana** |
| tire | **ponè, kodiàrana** |
| windshield | **pare-brise** *fr* |

## ◆ Loss and Robbery

In big towns beware of street crime, including muggings and purse snatchings. Night errands should be avoided. Do not be conspicuous with your belongings, such as camera equipment, money and jewelry.

It is prudent to lock the car from inside when driving around. Do not leave valuable things in the car.

Help!
>  **Vonjèo!**

Call the police!
>  **Miantsòa pôlìsy!**

Where is the police station?
>  **Àiza ny biràon'ny pôlìsy àho?**

Can I use your telephone?
>  **Àfaka mampiàsa ny telefàoninào àho ve?**

I am lost.
>  **Vèry àho.**

I want to contact my embassy.
>  **Mìla mirèsaka àmin'ny ny ambasàdiko àho.**

I need an interpreter.
>  **Mìla mpandìka tèny àho.**

My ... has been stolen.
>  **Nìsy nangàlatra ny ... ko.**

I lost my ... .
>  **Vèry ny ... ko.**

I have been robbed.
>  **Nìsy nanèndaka àho.**

I did not do that.
>  **Tsy nanào izàny àho.**

I need a lawyer.
>  **Mìla avocat àho.**

## Words

| | |
|---|---|
| bag | paokètra |
| camera | fàkan-tsàry |
| car | fiàra, fiàrakodìa, tômôbìlina |
| documents | taratàsy |
| eyeglasses | solomàso |
| I.D. | kàra-panòndro |
| interpreter | mpandìka tèny |
| key | lakilè |
| lawyer | avocat *fr* |
| lost | vèry |
| money | vòla |
| passport | pasipàoro |
| pickpocket | mpangàro-pàosy |
| police | pôlìsy |
| police station | biràon'ny pôlìsy |
| purse | fitoèram-bòla |
| stolen | nìsy nangàlatra |
| suitcase | valìzy |
| telephone | telefàonina |
| thief | mpangàlatra |
| ticket | biè |
| wallet | porte-feuille *fr* |
| watch | famantaranàndro |

Numbers

How many ... ?
   **Fìry ny ... ?**
Can you count the number of ... ?
   **Àfaka manìsa ny isàn'ny ... ve ianào?**

Notice the use of the linker **ambìn'ny** in the tens, and the use of **àmby** in combinations from twenty on.

In combinations 'one' is read **iràika** instead of **irày**.

| | |
|---|---|
| 0 | **àotra** |
| 1 | **irày, iràika** |
| 2 | **ròa** |
| 3 | **tèlo** |
| 4 | **èfatra** |
| 5 | **dìmy** |
| 6 | **ènina** |
| 7 | **fìto** |
| 8 | **vàlo** |
| 9 | **sìvy** |
| 10 | **fòlo** |
| | |
| 11 | **iràika ambìn'ny fòlo** |
| 12 | **ròa ambìn'ny fòlo** |
| 19 | **sìvy ambìn'ny fòlo** |
| 20 | **roapòlo** |
| 21 | **iràika àmby roapòlo** |
| 27 | **fìto àmby roapòlo** |
| 30 | **tèlopòlo** |
| 40 | **èfapòlo** |
| 50 | **dìmampòlo** |
| 60 | **ènimpòlo** |
| 70 | **fìtopòlo** |

| | |
|---|---|
| 80 | **vàlopòlo** |
| 90 | **sivifòlo** |
| 98 | **vàlo àmby sìvifòlo** |
| 99 | **sìvy àmby sìvifòlo** |
| 100 | **zàto** |
| 101 | **iràika àmby zàto** |
| 104 | **èfatra àmby zàto** |
| 200 | **ròanjàto** |
| 300 | **tèlonjàto** |
| 400 | **èfajàto** |
| 500 | **dimanjàto** |
| 600 | **èninjàto** |
| 700 | **sìvinjàto** |
| 800 | **vàlonjàto** |
| 900 | **sìvinjàto** |
| 1000 | **arìvo** |
| 10,000 | **irày àlina** |
| 100,000 | **irày hètsy** |
| 1,000,000 | **irày tapitrìsa** |

Ordinal numbers are built with **fàha-** followed by the cardinal number, with the exception of 'first':

| | |
|---|---|
| first | **voalòhany** |
| second | **fàharòa** |
| third | **fàhatèlo** |
| fourth | **fàhaèfatra** |
| tenth | **fàhafòlo** |
| fifteenth | **fàhadìmy ambìn'ny fòlo** |
| twentieth | **fàharoapòlo** |
| | |
| one-half | **antsàsany** |
| one-quarter | **ampahèfany** |
| three-quarters | **tèlo ampahèfany** |
| one-third | **ampàhatèlony** |
| two-thirds | **ròa ampàhatèlony** |

# NUMBERS

## WORDS

| | |
|---|---|
| number *n.* | **ìsa** |
| to add | **manàmpy** |
| to count | **manìsa** |
| to multiply | **mampitòmpo** |
| to substract | **manàla** |

Time

I am late.
> **Tàra àho.**

I am in a hurry.
> **Màika àho.**

My watch is ... minutes fast.
> **Avànsa ... minìtra ny famantaranàndroko.**

My watch is ... minutes late.
> **Tàra ... minìtra ny famantaranàndroko.**

My watch is broken.
> **Màty ny famantaranàndroko.**

What time is it?
> **Àmin'ny fìry izào?**

It is ... o'clock.
> **Àmin'ny ... .**

At what time?
> **Àmin'ny fìry?** (time in the future or at present)
> **Tàmin'ny fìry?** (time in the past)

At ... .
> **Àmin'ny ... .** (time in the future or at present)
> **Tàmin'ny ... .** (time in the past)

| | |
|---|---|
| one | **irày** |
| two | **ròa** |
| three | **tèlo** |
| four | **èfatra** |
| five | **dìmy** |
| six | **ènina** |
| seven | **fìto** |
| eight | **vàlo** |
| nine | **sìvy** |
| ten | **fòlo** |
| eleven | **iràika ambìn'ny fòlo** |
| twelve | **ròa ambìn'ny fòlo** |

It is two o'clock.
> **Àmin'ny ròa.**

It is 2:05.
> **Àmin'ny ròa sy dìmy.**

It is 2:15.
> **Àmin'ny ròa sy fahèfany.**

It is 2:18.
> **Àmin'ny ròa sy vàlo ambìn'ny fòlo minìtra.**

It is 2:30.
> **Àmin'ny ròa sy sàsany.**

It is 2:45.
> **Àmin'ny tèlo làtsaka fahèfany.**

It is 2:55.
> **Àmin'ny tèlo làtsaka dìmy.**

When? (time in the future)
> **Rahovìana?**

When? (time in the past)
> **Ovìana?**

## WORDS

| | |
|---|---|
| afternoon | **hàriva** |
| appointment | **fotòana vonjèna** |
| day | **àndro** |
| evening | **folakàndro** |
| fortnight | **tapa-bòlana** |
| hour | **òra** |
| in a few days | **àfaka àndro vitsivìtsy** |
| in the morning | **àmin'ny maràina** |
| in the afternoon/ evening | **àmin'ny harìva** |
| in the night | **àmin'ny àlina** |
| at noon | **àmin'ny atoàndro** |
| last ... | **tàmin'ny ...** |
| last week | **tàmin'ny herinàndro** |

| | |
|---|---|
| last month | **tàmin'ny irày vòlana làsa** |
| last year | **tàmin'ny herintàona** |
| midnight | **sasak'àlina** |
| minute | **minìtra** |
| month | **vòlana** |
| morning | **maràina** |
| next week | **àmin'ny herinàndro** |
| next month | **àmin'ny vòlana ambòny** |
| next year | **àmin'ny herintàona** |
| night | **àlina** |
| noon | **atoàndro** |
| now | **izào** |
| on (time in the future) | **àmin'ny ...** (days of the week) |
| on (time in the past) | **tàmin'ny ...** (days of the week) |
| second | **segòndra** |
| the day after tomorrow | **rahafakampìtso** |
| this morning | **anìo maràina** |
| this week | **àmin'ity herinàndro ity** |
| today | **anìo** |
| tomorrow | **rahampìtso** |
| watch | **famantaranàndro** |
| week | **herinàndro** |
| year | **tàona** |
| yesterday | **omàly** |

## Days of the Week

| | |
|---|---|
| Monday | **alatsinàiny** |
| Tuesday | **talàta** |
| Wednesday | **alarobìa** |
| Thursday | **alakamìsy** |
| Friday | **zomà** |
| Saturday | **asabòtsy** |
| Sunday | **alahàdy** |

### ◆ Weights and Measures

The metric system is used in Malagasy. The unit of weight or measurement is explicitly referred to in a question:

How deep is it?
**Fìry mètatra ny halàliny?**
How wide is it?
**Fìry mètatra ny sàkany?**
How heavy is it?
**Fìry kilào?**
Do you have a scale?
**Mànana fandan-jàna ve ianào?**

### ◆ Weight

| | |
|---|---|
| gram | **gràma** |
| kilogram | **kilôgràma/kilào** (2.2 pounds) |
| half a kilogram | **antsàsany** |
| a quarter kilogram | **fahèfany** |
| heavy | **mavèsatra** |
| light | **màivana** |

### ◆ Volume

| | |
|---|---|
| square meter | **mètatra tòra-dròa** |
| liter | **lìtatra** (2.1 pints) |

### ◆ Distance

| | |
|---|---|
| centimeter | **santimètatra** |
| meter | **mètatra** |
| kilometer | **kilômètatra** (1 mile = 1.6 kilometers) |
| far | **làvitra** |
| near | **akàiky** |
| deep | **làlina** |

## ◆ Colors

What color is this?
   **Ìnona ity lòko ity?**
I do not like this color.
   **Tsy tìako ity lòko ity.**
I like ... .
   **... no tìako.**
I prefer the ... one.
   **... no tìako kokòa.**
My favorite color is ... .
   **... no lòko tìako indrìndra.**
This is too dark.
   **Màtroka lòatra ity.**
Does it come in a different color?
   **Mìsy lòko hàfa ve ity?**

### WORDS

| | |
|---|---|
| black | **màinty** |
| blackish | **maintimàinty** |
| blue | **mangà** |
| bluish | **mangamànga** |
| brown | **vòlon-tàny** |
| color | **lòko** |
| colored | **milòko** |
| colorful | **marèvaka** |
| dark | **màtroka** |
| golden | **mivòlom-bolamèna** |
| gray | **vòlon-tàny** |
| green | **màintso** |
| light | **tanòra** |
| orange | **vòlom-boasàry** |
| pink | **màvokèly** |
| purple | **vòlom-paràsy** |

# COLORS

| | |
|---|---|
| red | **mèna** |
| reddish | **menamèna** |
| silver | **mirànom-bolafòtsy** |
| striped | **mitsipitsìpika** |
| white | **fòtsy** |
| with dots | **mipentipèntina** |
| yellow | **màvo** |
| yellowish | **mavomàvo** |

## ◆ Facts on Madagascar

**Madagascar:** the world's fourth largest island after Greenland, New Guinea and Borneo.

**Location:** 250 miles off the southeast coast of Africa, extends 1,000 miles in length and 360 miles at its largest width.

**Government:** republic

**Surface area:** 587,041 sq. km

**Capital city:** Antananarivo, also called Tananarive *fr*

**Population:** 14,873,000 (1999 est.)
**Population growth rate:** 2,8% (1999 est.)

**Religions:** traditional beliefs (ancestors' devotion) 52%, Christian 41%, Muslim 7%

**Climate:** The climate throughout the island is moderated by altitude, with the coast being hotter (average temperature 21°–26°C or 70°–80°F) and wetter than the central plateau (average temperature 13°–19.4°C, 55°–67°F).
  Along the coast: tropical mountain climate
  Inland: temperate, rain from the monsoon
      winds during the austral summer (October
      to April)
  In the south: arid
  In the east: heavy rain during the austral winter
      (May to September)
  In the west: sheltered from trade winds, very
      light rain

# FACTS ON MADAGASCAR

**Visa:** Travelers going to Madagascar require a visa. These are issued at the Malagasy Embassy or Honorary Consulate:

> In the U.S.: Washington, DC (Embassy) or New York, NY (UN Mission)
>
> In the U.K.: London or Newcastle (Honorary Consulate)
>
> In Kenya: Nairobi (Honorary Consulate)

**Main public holidays:**

> January 1 — New Year's Day
> March 29 — Commemoration Day
> May 1 — Workers' Day
> May 24 — OAU Day
> June 26 — Independence Day
> November 1 — All Saints Day
> December 25 — Christmas Day
> December 30 — Republic Day
> Movable holidays: Good Friday, Easter Monday

**Electricity:** 110 volts and 220 volts. Electric outlets match the French standard.

**Banking hours:** Monday - Friday: 8 A.M.-4 P.M.
**Business hours** (including shops): Monday - Saturday 8 A.M.-12 P.M. and 2 P.M.-6 P.M.

**Local time:** +3 hours GMT

MADAGASCAR

# DICTIONARY AND PHRASEBOOKS

**Albanian-English/English-Albanian**
2,000 entries • 186 pages • 3¾ x 7
ISBN 0-7818-0793-X • $11.95pb • (498)

**Arabic-English/English-Arabic
(Eastern Arabic)**
2,200 entries • 142 pages • 3¾ x 7
ISBN 0-7818-0685-2 • $11.95pb • (774)

**Australian-English/English-Australian**
1,500 entries • 131 pages • 3¾ x 7
ISBN 0-7818-0539-2 • $11.95pb • (626)

**Azerbaijani-English/English-Azerbaijani**
2,000 entries • 176 pages • 3¾ x 7
ISBN 0-7818-0684-4 • $11.95pb • (753)

**Basque-English/English-Basque**
1,500 entries • 206 pages • 3¾ x 7
ISBN 0-7818-0622-4 • $11.95pb • (751)

**Bosnian-English/English-Bosnian**
1,500 entries • 171 pages • 3¾ x 7
ISBN 0-7818-0596-1 • $11.95pb • (691)

**Breton-English/English-Breton**
1,500 entries • 176 pages • 3¾ x 7
ISBN 0-7818-0540-6 • $11.95pb • (627)

**British-American/American-British English**
1,400 entries • 154 pages • 3¾ x 7
ISBN 0-7818-0450-7 • $11.95pb • (247)

**Chechen-English/English-Chechen**
1,400 entries • 176 pages • 3¾ x 7
ISBN 0-7818-0446-9 • $11.95pb • (183)

**Croatian-English/English-Croatian**
2,000 entries • 272 pages • 3¾ x 7
ISBN 0-7818-0810-3 • $11.95pb • (111)

**English-Ilocano**
7,000 entries • 269 pages • 5½ x 8½
ISBN 0-7818-0642-9 • $14.95pb • (718)

**Esperanto-English/English-Esperanto**
2,500 entries • 223 pages • 3¾ x 7
ISBN 0-7818-0736-0 • $13.95pb • (309)

**French-English/English-French**
2,000 entries • 175 pages • 3¾ x 7
ISBN 0-7818-0856-1 • $11.95pb • (128)

**Georgian-English/English-Georgian**
1,300 entries • 150 pages • 3¾ x 7
ISBN 0-7818-0542-2 • $11.95pb • (630)

**German-English/English-German**
4,000 entries • 180 pages • 3¾ x 7
ISBN 0-7818-0857-X • $12.95pb • (148)

**Greek-English/English-Greek**
1,500 entries • 263 pages • 3¾ x 7
ISBN 0-7818-0635-6 • $14.95pb • (715)

**Hebrew-English/English-Hebrew**
*Romanized*
2,000 entries • 180 pages • 3¾ x 7
ISBN 0-7818-0811-1 • $11.95pb • (126)

**Igbo-English/English-Igbo**
2,500 entries • 186 pages • 3¾ x 7
ISBN 0-7818-0661-5 • $11.95pb • (750)

**Irish-English/English-Irish**
1,400 entries • 71 pages • 3¾ x 7
ISBN 0-87052-110-1 • $7.95pb • (385)

**Italian-English/English-Italian**
2,100 entries • 213 pages • 3¾ x 7
ISBN 0-7818-0812-X • $11.95pb • (137)

**Japanese-English/English-Japanese**
*Romanized*
2,300 entries • 220 pages • 3¾ x 7
ISBN 0-7818-0814-6 • $12.95pb • (205)

**Lao-English/English-Lao**
*Romanized*
2,500 entries • 198 pages • 3¾ x 7
ISBN 0-7818-0858-8 • $12.95pb • (179)

**Lingala-English/English-Lingala**
2,200 entries • 120 pages • 3 _ x 7
ISBN 0-7818-0456-6 • $11.95pb • (296)

**Maltese-English/English-Maltese**
1,500 entries • 175 pages • 3¾ x 7
ISBN 0-7818-0565-1 • $11.95pb • (697)

**Maya-English/English-Maya (Yucatec)**
1,500 entries • 180 pages • 3¾ x 7
ISBN 0-7818-0859-6 • $12.95pb • (244)

**Pilipino-English/English-Pilipino (Tagalog)**
2,200 entries • 186 pages • 3¾ x 7
ISBN 0-7818-0451-5 • $11.95pb • (295)

**Polish-English/English-Polish**
6,000 entries • 252 pages • 5½ x 8½
ISBN 0-7818-0134-6 • $11.95pb • (192)

**Romansch-English/English-Romansch**
1,800 entries • 193 pages • 5½ x 7
ISBN 0-7818-0778-6 • $12.95pb • (316)

**Russian-English/English-Russian**
*Revised*
3,000 entries • 228 pages • 5½ x 8½
ISBN 0-7818-0190-7 • $11.95pb • (597)

**Shona-English/English-Shona**
1,400 entries • 160 pages • 3¾ x 7
ISBN 0-7818-0813-8 • $11.95pb • (167)

**Slovak-English/English-Slovak**
1,300 entries • 180 pages • 3¾ x 7
ISBN 0-7818-0663-1 • $13.95pb • (754)

**Somali-English/English-Somali**
1,400 entries • 176 pages • 3¾ x 7
ISBN 0-7818-0621-6 • $13.95pb • (755)

**Spanish-English/English-Spanish
(Latin American)**
2,000 entries • 250 pages • 3¾ x 7
ISBN 0-7818-0773-5 • $11.95pb • (261)

**Tajik-English/English-Tajik**
1,400 entries • 200 pages • 3¾ x 7
ISBN 0-7818-0662-3 • $11.95pb • (752)

**Thai-English/English-Thai**
*Romanized*
1,800 entries • 197 pages • 3¾ x 7
ISBN 0-7818-0774-3 • $12.95pb • (330)

**Ukrainian-English/English-Ukrainian**
3,000 entries • 205 pages • 5½ x 8½
ISBN 0-7818-0188-5 • $11.95pb • (28)

Prices subject to change without prior notice. To order
**Hippocrene Books**, contact your local bookstore, call
(718) 454-2366, visit www.hippocrenebooks.com, or write
to: Hippocrene Books, 171 Madison Ave., New York, NY
10016. Please enclose check or money order adding $5.00
shipping (UPS) for the first book and $.50 for each addi-
tional title.